michaelHR
United Kingdom HR, untangled.



A PRACTICAL GUIDE TO:

# UK EMPLOYMENT LAW

FIRST EDITION

For HR Professionals, Managers & Employees

By Michael Bear ACIPD

MICHAELHR.COM

# ACKNOWLEDGEMENTS

The journey of writing "A Practical Guide To: UK Employment Law" has been a blend of late nights, endless cups of coffee, daunting challenges, and exciting triumphs. Every word written, every concept explored, has been a step forward in a journey made possible by the unwavering support of those around me.

First and foremost, to my rock, my husband Mark—your unfailing faith in my abilities transformed late-night sessions of doubt into mornings of triumph. Your patient explanation of complex concepts during my most frustrating moments provided the clarity needed to progress. To my mother, Susan, your strength and resilience through life's challenges have always inspired me. Your unwavering support was my guiding light, particularly during the gruelling editing phase.

I sincerely thank the University of London, particularly Jack Dybczak and Dr. Keely Jo Frasca. Jack, your insightful feedback helped refine my thoughts, while Dr. Frasca's challenging questions pushed me to delve deeper into each topic.

A special thank you to my HR colleagues across the UK, who generously shared their innovative practices and invaluable experiences. Your insights have transformed this book from a simple guide into a comprehensive resource for employees, employers, and HR practitioners. And finally, to you, the reader, for choosing to embark on this journey with me. I hope this book is your trusted companion in navigating the complexities of UK employment law. Should you have any feedback for future editions of this book, my email is michael.bear@michaelhr.com.



First Edition (Paperback): Published October 2023.

ISBN: 978-1-3999-6630-6

# INTRODUCTION

UK employment law is akin to a dense, mystifying forest, teeming with complexities and potential snares that are often challenging to navigate. A labyrinthine landscape of legal terminologies and procedural protocols can quickly leave one feeling adrift and bewildered. I, too, grappled with this disconcerting sense when first delving into the domain of employment law. This struggle spurred me to write "A Practical Guide To: UK Employment Law".

Imagine the confidence to cross this daunting forest armed with a reliable compass. As an entrepreneur, this understanding would empower you to establish a just and productive work environment, bolstering your company's reputation. As a manager, this knowledge would equip you with the skills to handle human resources-related issues with ease and proficiency. This is the transformative power that a sound understanding and accurate application of UK employment law can grant.

In the forthcoming chapters, we embark on an in-depth exploration of various aspects of employment law. Our discussion will be enriched with practical examples, helpful tips, and common challenges encountered across diverse work contexts. The book will also shed light on the nuances of employment law as they apply to different types of employment, whether full-time, part-time, temporary, or freelance.

Whether you are a novice trying to get a foothold in this field or someone with a rudimentary understanding striving to broaden your knowledge base, this book promises to be your steadfast ally. It will guide you through the intricate maze of UK employment law, untangling the complexities and equipping you with the knowledge to navigate this challenging domain effectively.

As we advance, we will encounter the thorny issues of dispute resolution and tribunal procedures. The spectre of legal action often looms in these areas, casting long shadows of uncertainty and apprehension. However, fear not! This guide will elucidate the intricacies of procedural norms, untangling the process and illuminating the path to resolution. We will examine the steps involved, the rights and responsibilities of each party, and the potential outcomes, equipping you with the knowledge to handle such situations with confidence and composure.

With this guide, you will survive and thrive in the challenging yet rewarding world of UK employment law. Our journey does not end here; instead, it is a continual process of learning and growth. So, let us stride forward, ready to conquer the challenges and seize the opportunities.

**Are you ready to embark on this journey?**

# CONTENTS

Hampstead Heath
24

# JOIN THE HRUK REDDIT COMMUNITY

While searching for HR news on Reddit in late 2017, I soon realised something needed to be dedicated to professionals in the UK's human resources. r/humanresources actively catered to a predominantly US audience, with content reflective of its US membership. This landscape made seeking UK-specific talking points, with Reddit's signature approach to conversation, a challenge. I created r/HumanResourcesUK to meet this challenge.

This was not a commercial idea. The goal was to create a virtual panoply where other HR professionals in the UK could gather to discover new ideas and resources—a space intended to flourish organically with the collective wisdom and experience of many UK HR minds. The strategy was a success.

Today, r/HumanResourcesUK has over 2,600 members, with contemporary topics and active discussion threads covering all areas of UK HR. Moderation is kept to a minimum, with the only significant rule being that discussion is respectful discussion at all times and promotion of commercial software and services is forbidden. Members can also flag posts they do not feel belong in the community for review.

Every week, the subreddit is visited by hundreds of people from across the UK and worldwide seeking advice on strategy or HR matters. The community welcomes HR professionals and is a valuable forum for managers and employees.

HRUK

**VISIT THE COMMUNITY**

You can visit the HRUK Reddit community by scanning the code below with your phone camera. Alternatively, visit: https://reddit.com/r/HumanResourcesUK

Shepherd's Bush 148
LONDON UNITED
LT141

# CHAPTER 1
# AN OVERVIEW OF UK EMPLOYMENT LAW

# DEFINITION & SCOPE

UK employment law, a comprehensive and dynamic body of legal rules, plays a pivotal role in shaping the workplace environment in the United Kingdom. This legal system encapsulates several aspects of the employment relationship, ensuring a fair, equal, and respectful professional landscape. Regarding recruitment, UK employment law mandates that employers maintain transparency and fairness throughout the process. This includes providing complete and accurate job descriptions, setting unbiased selection criteria, and eliminating any form of preference or discrimination. For instance, a potential employer cannot favour a candidate based on their age, race, gender, or any other personal characteristic. This law ensures everyone has a fair shot at employment opportunities.

The law establishes working conditions standards for working hours, rest periods, and minimum wage. It protects employees from unfair exploitation and provides a healthy work-life balance. Furthermore, it safeguards employees from wrongful termination by requiring employers to have a valid reason and follow due process before dismissing an employee.

UK employment law takes a strong stance against workplace discrimination and harassment. It mandates equal treatment for all employees, regardless of race, age, gender, religion, or disability. Employers are legally obliged to maintain a safe working environment and implement measures to prevent accidents and injuries.

In addition, UK employment law covers various employee benefits, including holiday pay, sick pay, maternity and paternity leave, pension schemes. It also guides processes for redundancies or business transfers, ensuring they are executed fairly and transparently. Under this law, employees' rights are safeguarded even when the ownership of the workplace changes.

Comprehension and adherence to these laws are crucial for a harmonious workplace. Employers can achieve this through regular legal training sessions or consultations with employment law specialists. On the other hand, employees can consider joining trade unions or seeking advice from legal professionals or advisory bodies to stay informed about their rights.

However, the practical application of these laws may vary depending on several factors, including the individual circumstances of each case, the interpretation and enforcement of the laws, and the effectiveness of the relevant institutions in upholding these laws.

To stay updated with the latest changes in the law, employers and employees need to actively engage with legal updates, participate in workshops or seminars, or subscribe to legal news platforms. Employers should also consider implementing anti-discrimination policies, regular workplace inspections, and training programs on workplace ethics to ensure a safe and discrimination-free workplace.

**DID YOU KNOW?**

UK employment law is a dynamic entity, continually evolving and adapting due to the introduction of new legislation, amendments to existing laws, or shifts in legal precedents set by court judgments. This ongoing evolution makes it a complex and critical area that requires constant attention and understanding.

New legislation often emerges in response to societal changes, technological advancements, or political shifts. For example, laws may be introduced to address issues related to remote work, digital security, or diversity and inclusion in the workplace. Such legislation is often implemented to ensure that the workplace adapts to these changes and offers employees a fair and safe environment.

Amendments to existing laws are another key driver of changes in employment law. These amendments are often made to improve, refine, or modernise existing legislation. They might involve changes to regulations regarding working hours, minimum wage rates, or employee benefits. These amendments reflect the changing needs and expectations of the workforce, as well as shifts in economic conditions or government policy.

# TYPES OF EMPLOYMENT CONTRACT

Before we explore the key areas of UK employment law, it is essential to note fundamental employment rights vary depending on the type of employment contract. There are six main types of employment contracts under UK law.

**Full-Time**

UK law terms individuals employed under this type of contract as 'employees'. They have the right to the National Minimum Wage (NMW), paid annual leave, rest breaks, protection against unjust termination, redundancy compensation, and the ability to ask for adaptable work schedules after 26 weeks of service. In addition, 'employees' are entitled to maternity, paternity, adoption or shared parental leave and pay, ensuring they can maintain work-life balance during significant life events.

They are also entitled to statutory sick pay, offering financial support during ill health, thus fostering a supportive working environment.

**Part-Time**

Employees under this type of contract enjoy the same rights as their full-time counterparts on a pro-rata basis, including paid annual leave and at least the NMW. They usually work fewer hours, and their schedules can fluctuate. UK law protects part-time employees from receiving less favourable treatment than full-time employees. Despite their reduced hours, part-time employees are eligible for the same benefits as full-time employees, such as pension contributions and maternity leave. Their work pattern may vary weekly, but they should not be excluded from company training or promotional opportunities merely due to their part-time status.

**Fixed-Term**

Employees working under fixed-term contracts enjoy rights identical to those of permanent employees. Under UK law, when an employer renews a fixed-term contract multiple times or if an employee serves under a fixed-term contract for four or more years, the employee may qualify as a 'permanent employee' under specific conditions.

Furthermore, the transition from a fixed-term to a permanent contract should be seamless and not infringe on the employee's existing rights. Employers must understand that this automatic transition does not require additional documentation or formal procedures, ensuring the employee's service and benefits continuity.

**Zero-Hours**

UK law classifies individuals employed on zero-hour contracts as 'workers'. They have the right to the NMW, paid annual leave, rest breaks, and protection against discrimination.

However, 'workers' on zero-hour contracts might enjoy different job security or guaranteed hours than 'employees'. Workers under zero-hour contracts are entitled to statutory sick pay and protection against unlawful dismissal. Yet, the flexibility of these contracts means that the predictability of their income can vary, potentially leading to financial instability.

**Contractor / Freelancer**

UK law typically recognises freelancers and contractors as 'self-employed', which means they might not enjoy the same rights and protections as 'employees'. However, they hold more control over their working conditions and can negotiate their contracts.

They also have protection against discrimination. By being self-employed, freelancers and contractors also have the flexibility to decide on the number of clients they work with, further diversifying their work portfolio.

They have the freedom to set their hours and location of work, providing them with a unique work-life balance that is often unavailable to traditional employees.

**Apprenticeship**

UK law recognises apprentices as 'employees' with the same rights as other employees. These rights include earning at least the NMW for apprentices if they are under 19 or over 19 and in their first year. After this, they qualify for the minimum wage appropriate to their age.

Apprentices are also entitled to work in a safe and healthy environment, with all necessary training and supervision provided by the employer. Furthermore, they are granted paid leave sick pay and can operate standard working hours in line with employment legislation.

# EMPLOYMENT RIGHTS

In the UK, employment rights represent a comprehensive array of protections and entitlements specifically engineered to promote the welfare of those in the workforce. These rights, established for fair treatment, protect employees nationwide, shielding them from potential workplace injustices.

**Power of the Written Contract**

A fundamental component of these rights is the mandatory existence of a written employment contract. This document is a detailed exposé of the precise terms and conditions governing an individual's employment. It generally encompasses critical information such as the job description, expected working hours, details of remuneration, and the enumeration of any additional perks or benefits. The contract operates as a legal provision, safeguarding the interests of both parties involved—the employer and the employee.

**OWN GOAL**

In the 1993 case of Tottenham Hotspur Plc v Venables, involving football manager Terry Venables, Venables' contract stated that they could not dismiss him without cause. When the club tried to fire him, he took them to court for breach of contract.

The court ruled in Venables' favour, reinforcing the power of a written agreement.

**Employment Rights Act 1996**

The Employment Rights Act 1996, a landmark legislation in UK labour law, ensures that those with 'employee' status are entitled to a written statement explaining the main terms and conditions of their employment provided by their employer. This act is instrumental in fostering transparency and mutual understanding within the employment relationship, thereby reducing potential disputes and misunderstandings.

**National Minimum Wage Act 1998**

Remuneration forms a critical element of employment rights in the UK. This Act made it a statutory requirement for those with 'employee' or 'worker (limb b)' status to receive at least the National Minimum Wage (NMW). The National Minimum Wage Act 1998 governs this principle, stipulating that the minimum wage rate differs depending on the employee's age and apprentice status. This law is indispensable in ensuring a basic standard of living for all working individuals in the UK.

**Working Time Regulations 1998**

Those with 'employee' or 'worker (limb b)' status have a statutory right to paid leave. The Working Time Regulations 1998 guarantees workers are entitled to 5.6 weeks of paid holiday each calendar year. This provision allows workers to enjoy necessary rest periods without financial strain, contributing significantly to their overall mental and physical well-being.

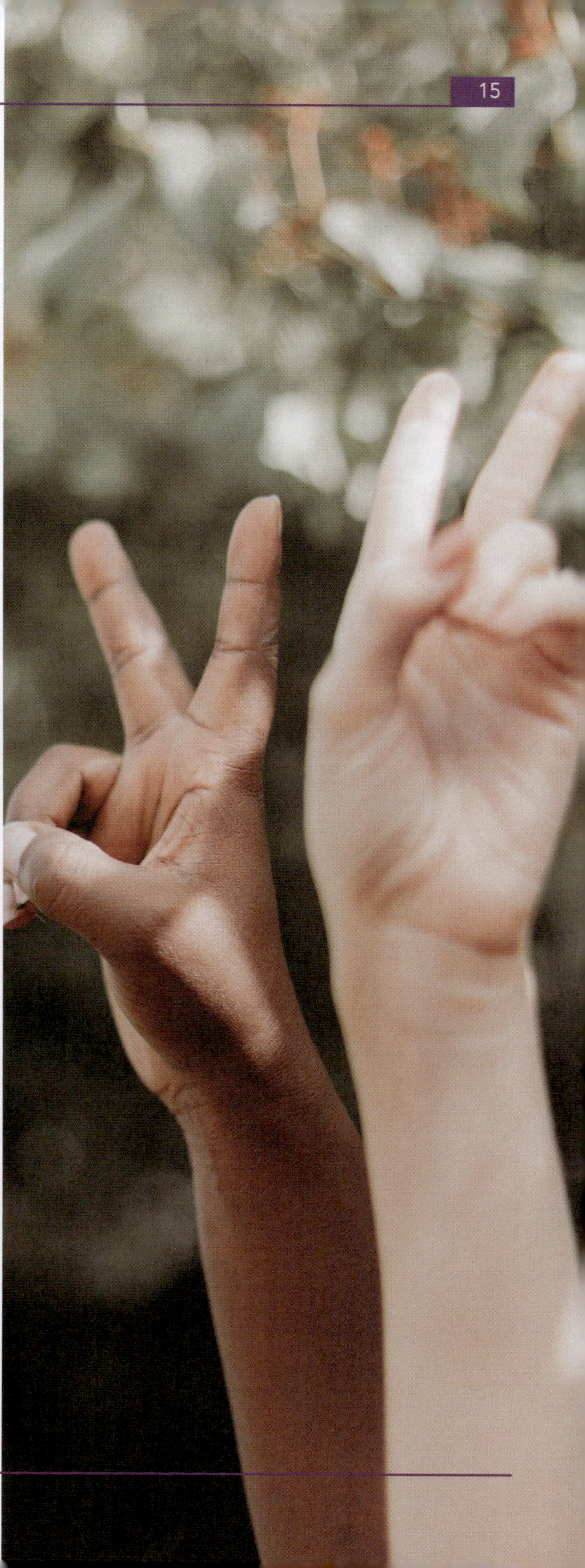

**Variations in Employment Contracts**

While these are fundamental employment rights, it is crucial to acknowledge they can vary based on the employment contract type. For instance, entitlements may differ for those on permanent, fixed-term, part-time, or zero-hours contracts. There are also rights to maternity and paternity leave, protection against unjust dismissal, and the right to flexible working arrangements. Each of these variations strives to create an inclusive work environment that respects the needs of those with 'employee' or 'worker (limb b)' status.

**CHECKS & (DUE) BALANCES**

In 2016, UK retailer Sports Direct was investigated by HMRC for underpaying workers, as mandatory security checks pushed their basic wage below the National Minimum Wage.

The case was resolved with Sports Direct being required to pay approximately £1m back wages to their underpaid employees. This landmark case served as a potent reminder to all employers about the importance of considering all required duties when calculating pay. It also highlighted the need for employers to ensure that their practices align with legal requirements, particularly regarding the National Minimum Wage. Failure to abide by these regulations can result in significant financial and reputational damage.

# DISCRIMINATION LAW

UK employment law has comprehensive standards and regulations to prevent discrimination and promote workplace equality. The cornerstone of these legislations is the Equality Act 2010, which covers a broad spectrum of protected characteristics, including age, gender, race, religion, disability, and sexual orientation. This legislation applies at all stages of employment, from the initial job application and interview process to the termination of employment, including redundancies.

To illustrate its practical implications, let us consider a few scenarios. Suppose you are an older worker approaching retirement age. The Equality Act ensures that an employer cannot reject your job application solely based on age. This law element is designed to foster age diversity and fairness in the workplace, asserting that job opportunities should be as open to you as they are to younger individuals, like recent graduates.

The Equality Act 2010 also seeks financial equity and gender equality in the workplace. For instance, if you are a woman in the same role as a man, the law stipulates that you both should receive equal pay. This principle, first established in the Equal Pay Act of 1970, has been incorporated into the Equality Act 2010, reinforcing the commitment to gender equality in remuneration.

Furthermore, suppose you are an employee with a disability. In that case, the law mandates your employer to make reasonable adjustments to accommodate your needs. This could range from providing specialised equipment or altering your working hours to physically modifying the workplace. This provision is integral to creating an inclusive work environment that is fair and equitable for all, irrespective of physical abilities or constraints.

Despite the robust framework of the UK's discrimination laws, they can only partially prevent discrimination. This is because lapses in enforcement or lack of awareness can still lead to instances of discrimination. Thus, the effectiveness of these protective laws often hinges on the action and understanding of both employers and employees. Navigating this complex landscape can be challenging, but with the correct information and support, every worker can assert their rights and contribute to a fair and inclusive workplace.

**DID YOU KNOW?**

The Equality Act of 2010, a cornerstone of UK employment law, was a significant legislative milestone. It integrated and streamlined more than 100 separate pieces of legislation into a comprehensive single Act.

Some of the main pieces of legislation incorporated into the Act include the Equal Pay Act 1970, The Sex Discrimination Act of 1975, The Race Relations Act of 1976 and the The Disability Discrimination Act of 1995.

# TYPES OF DISCRIMINATION

**Direct Discrimination**

Direct discrimination refers to a situation in which an individual is treated less favourably than others in similar circumstances because of a protected characteristic. In the context of UK employment law, these characteristics could include age, gender, race, disability, religion or belief, sexual orientation, marriage or civil partnership status, pregnancy or maternity. For instance, if an employer refuses to hire a competent applicant solely because of their racial background, this is a clear example of direct discrimination.

**Indirect Discrimination**

Indirect discrimination occurs when a seemingly neutral policy, rule, or procedure, which applies to everyone equally, has a disproportionate and disadvantageous impact on specific individuals because of a protected characteristic they possess. For example, a business introduces a policy that all employees must have at least ten years of experience in a similar role. This could indirectly discriminate against younger people who might not have had the opportunity to gain such lengthy expertise due to their age.

**Harassment**

Harassment encompasses any unwanted behaviour linked to a protected characteristic that creates an intimidating, hostile, degrading, humiliating or offensive environment for the individual. This can encompass various behaviours, including offensive jokes, derogatory comments, or unwanted physical contact.

**Victimisation**

Victimisation refers to treating an individual unjustly because they have lodged or supported a complaint about discrimination or harassment. An example would be an employee receiving unfair treatment or being ostracised after reporting incidents of sexual harassment in the workplace.

**Discrimination by Perception**

This form of discrimination transpires when an individual is treated less favourably based on the assumption that they possess a protected characteristic, regardless of whether they do or not. For example, an employee could be discriminated against because they are perceived as LGBTQ+.

**Discrimination by Association**

Discrimination by association happens when an individual faces discrimination because they are connected to another person with a protected characteristic. For instance, an employee could face discrimination because their child has a disability.

**Failure to Make Reasonable Adjustments**

This discrimination arises when an employer or service provider neglects to make necessary modifications to eliminate obstacles for a person with a disability. For example, an employer might not provide a disabled employee with an accessible workspace or allow flexible working hours, thereby discriminating against the individual. It is essential to note that under the Equality Act 2010, employers must make these reasonable adjustments to ensure equal opportunities.

# HEALTH & SAFETY

UK regulations mandate that all employers are accountable for providing their employees with a safe and healthy working environment. Specific laws, the Health and Safety at Work Act 1974 and the Management of Health and Safety at Work Regulations 1999, establish this responsibility.

The first step is to educate the workforce about potential hazards within their workplace. Comprehensive safety training programmes are effective for this, covering various topics, from identifying and mitigating risks to adequately using safety equipment and following established safety protocols. Besides providing education, employers must provide suitable work equipment and keep it in good condition. Regular inspections and servicing of machinery, tools, and other equipment are vital to this requirement, ensuring that the equipment is up to safety standards and free from defects that could cause accidents.

Maintaining a safe environment relies on risk assessments. Employers should conduct these risk assessments regularly and systematically, identify potential hazards, and take necessary steps to minimise associated risks.

**Measures include:**

- Conducting health and safety training.
- Updating ventilation systems.
- Ensuring availability of sanitary facilities.
- Enforcing stricter procedures as necessary.
- Maintaining workplace equipment.

Health and safety requirements may vary according to the nature of the job. Roles involving physical labour or handling hazardous materials may require more stringent safety measures than office-based roles. However, the fundamental principle of ensuring a safe and healthy working environment remains constant across all forms of employment.

Employers are responsible for these health and safety measures, and employees have duties under the Health and Safety at Work, etc. Act 1974. Individuals must care for their health and safety and those of others influenced by their actions. They also need to collaborate with their employers, enabling them to fulfil their legal obligations.

Businesses may face severe consequences, ranging from hefty fines to legal action, if they do not comply with these regulations. Furthermore, it can negatively impact a company's reputation among employees, customers, and the wider public. Therefore, holding these standards is in every employer's best interest, contributing to a safer, healthier working environment.

Employers must also consider their employees' mental well-being to ensure a safe and healthy working environment. Workplace stress can be as harmful as physical hazards. The Management of Health and Safety at Work Regulations 1999 requires employers to assess the risk of stress-related ill health arising from work activities. Employers can implement regular breaks, flexible working hours, and access to counselling services to manage employee stress levels. Creating an open and supportive work culture can also enable employees to speak up about any stress or mental health issues they are experiencing.

In addition to physical and mental health, the modern workplace must also consider the impact of technology on health and safety. With the advent of digital technologies, new risks such as repetitive strain injuries, eye strain, and cybersecurity threats have emerged. Employers should provide ergonomically designed workstations and regular screen breaks to minimise the risk of physical health problems. Employers must ensure robust security protocols and employees are trained to identify and respond to potential cyber threats.

Finally, employers should foster a culture of continuous improvement in health and safety. This involves regularly reviewing and updating safety protocols, providing refresher training, and encouraging employees to share their ideas and concerns about health and safety. To remain compliant, employers should also stay abreast of health and safety legislation changes. Regular health and safety audits can also help to identify areas for improvement. Remember that a safe and healthy workplace is not a destination but a journey that requires ongoing commitment and effort from employers and employees.

**DID YOU KNOW?**

The 2013 Regulations for Reporting Injuries, Diseases, and Dangerous Occurrences (RIDDOR) obligates employers and others who manage work locations to file reports on severe occupational incidents, health conditions related to work, and certain hazardous events.

# DISMISSAL & REDUNDANCY

In the UK, employment law governs the relationship between employers and employees, defining their rights, responsibilities, and protections. Two critical aspects of this relationship are dismissal and redundancy, which refer to terminating an employment contract. Dismissal is when an employer ends an individual's employment, while redundancy occurs when an employer reduces their workforce because a job or jobs have ceased. Specific legal procedures regulate both processes to ensure fairness and transparency.

**Dismissal Process:**

**1.** Written Reasons: If an employee has been continuously employed for more than one month, they have the right to receive a written statement of reasons for dismissal if they request one.

**2.** Notice Periods: Employees are entitled to a minimum notice period before their employment ends, known as statutory notice. The length varies from one week for those employed between one month and two years up to a maximum of 12 weeks for those employed for 12 years or more.

**3.** Right to Appeal: The employee can appeal the decision to dismiss them. This should be done in writing, stating the grounds of appeal.

**Redundancy Process**

**1.** Selection: The employer must use a fair and objective way of selecting employees to be made redundant. Commonly used methods include last in, first out (employees with the shortest length of service are selected first), asking for volunteers (self-selection), or scoring employees against a set of objective criteria (such as skills, qualifications, and experience).

**2.** Consultation: Employers must consult with employees (and their representatives, if applicable) before making redundancies. If 20 or more redundancies are being made, the consultation must start at least 30 days before any dismissals take effect. If 100 or more redundancies are being made, the consultation must begin at least 45 days before.

**3.** Notice and Pay: Employees selected for redundancy are usually entitled to statutory redundancy pay if they have been with their current employer for two years or more. The amount is based on their age, weekly income and length of service. They are also entitled to a notice period, the length of which depends on their length of service.

**4.** Alternative Employment: Employers should try to find alternative employment within the same company for employees who are being made redundant.

**5.** Time Off to Find a New Job: Employees who have been continuously employed for two years at the end of their notice period are entitled to a reasonable amount of time off to look for another job or to arrange training to help them find another job.

# TYPES OF DISMISSAL

**Fair Dismissal**

When an employee is dismissed for a valid reason, and the employer carries out the dismissal process reasonably, it is termed a fair dismissal. Valid reasons could include persistent underperformance, significant misconduct, redundancy, or any legal impediment preventing employees from fulfilling their work obligations. For instance, an employee who works as a delivery driver losing their driving license would constitute a legitimate reason for dismissal.

**Unfair Dismissal**

Unfair dismissal is a situation where an employee is let go without a valid reason or a fair process being followed. This can include conditions where the employer does not allow the employee to present their case or appeal the decision. For example, an employee dismissed based on unfounded allegations without an investigation may be considered unfair dismissal. Employers must adhere to the ACAS Code of Practice on Disciplinary and Grievance Procedures.

**Constructive Dismissal**

Constructive dismissal is when an employee feels compelled to resign due to their employer significantly breaching their employment contract. This could be related to a significant incident or a series of incidents, which makes it untenable for the employee to continue working. For instance, if an employer drastically changes the employee's role without their agreement, it may lead to a constructive dismissal claim.

**Wrongful Dismissal**

Wrongful dismissal is when an employer terminates an employee in violation of the terms of their contract. For example, if the employer fails to give the employee the correct notice period stipulated in their contract, it would be considered wrongful dismissal. In such cases, the employee could seek legal redress for breach of contract. The employee can file a claim with an employment tribunal for potential compensation.

**Summary Dismissal**

In instances of gross misconduct, an employee may be dismissed immediately without receiving a notice period or pay in place of notice. This is known as summary dismissal. Gross misconduct typically refers to severe breaches such as theft, physical violence or serious negligence, which results in significant loss / damage to the company.

**Redundancy**

Redundancy is a dismissal due to an employee's role becoming unnecessary, often from technological advancements, business decline, or halted operations in a particular area. The employer must ensure a fair redundancy process, including discussing with the employee, seeking other job opportunities, and offering appropriate redundancy compensation.

**Retirement Dismissal**

Before April 2011, employers in the UK had the right to enforce retirement at the age of 65, known as the Default Retirement Age. This is no longer supported.

# DATA PROTECTION

The Data Protection Act 2018 is a comprehensive piece of legislation in the UK that offers rigid guidelines about the collection, storage, and disposal of personal data, including employee data. This Act, which effectively mirrors the EU General Data Protection Regulation (GDPR), aims to maintain a high standard of data protection in light of the increasing digitalisation of personal information. One of the cornerstone principles of this law is the concept of 'data minimisation'. This principle compels employers to collect sufficient and pertinent information about their employees' roles and avoid excessive data collection. This data may encompass essential details such as an employee's home address, National Insurance number, bank account information for facilitating salary payments, and other crucial employment-related information.

Once this data has been procured, the Act imposes a legal responsibility on employers to guarantee its secure preservation. This can be achieved by applying stringent security measures such as data encryption to protect the data from potential hackers, access management controls to restrict and monitor who can access the data, and regular backup procedures to ensure data can be restored during a system failure.

The Data Protection Act 2018 stipulates that data should only be used for the purpose for which it was initially collected. An employer can only utilise an employee's data for unrelated activities, such as marketing if the employee has explicit permission. Therefore, organisations must establish precise data collection and usage policies, ensuring they comply with the law and respect the privacy rights of their employees.

Once the data has fulfilled its original purpose, the Act mandates its secure destruction. This could involve shredding paper documents or permanently deleting electronic records to thwart potential data recovery or misuse. Of course, there are exceptions to this rule, such as when the data is kept for legal requirements or for historical, statistical or research purposes.

The Act also grants a series of rights to employees regarding their data. They have the right to access their data, correct inaccuracies, object to processing in certain circumstances, and sometimes request data erasure. These rights are not absolute and will depend on the context and circumstances. Employers should be fully acquainted with these rights and establish suitable mechanisms to respond to employee requests promptly. Employee data should be treated with the highest level of respect, ensuring it is collected appropriately, stored securely, used responsibly and disposed of correctly, all while protecting the employee's privacy rights.

Failure to comply with the Data Protection Act 2018 can lead to significant penalties from the Information Commissioner's Office (ICO), which could result in substantial fines and severely tarnish the company's reputation. Hence, employers must comply wholly with the Act's provisions to avoid such repercussions.

# KEY CONCEPTS OF DATA SECURITY

**Encryption**

This is the process of converting data into a code using a secret key to prevent unauthorised access. Both stored data (data at rest) and data being sent over a network (data in transit) can be encrypted.

**Backup & Recovery**

Regular data backup, a crucial part of data management, provides a restore point for data during incidents like hardware or system failures and cyber attacks, with an effective system often encompassing daily backups and offsite storage for disaster recovery.

**Access Controls**

Access control refers to the selective restriction of access to sensitive data. This process involves identifying who is authorised to view, use, or modify the data.

**Firewalls**

These are security systems that monitor and control incoming and outgoing network traffic based on predetermined security rules. They form a barrier between a trusted internal network and untrusted external networks.

**Antivirus Software**

Antivirus software is a program designed to safeguard a computer or network from malware, including viruses, worms, and trojans. It does this by scanning for, detecting, and removing threats from the system.

**Intrusion Detection Systems (IDS)**

An Intrusion Detection System (IDS) is a tool that identifies suspicious activity or policy breaches within a network or system rather than blocking or filtering content like a firewall. It scrutinises network traffic and triggers an alert upon detecting irregularities that could signify a cyberattack. Some sophisticated IDS variants can even initiate proactive measures to halt an ongoing intrusion.

**Data Masking**

Data masking involves concealing specific data within a database record to create a version has the same structure but does not contain sensitive information. An example of this may be to conceal most of an employee's email address—for example 'm*******@gmail.com'. Masking can be combined with access controls to tailor visibility.

**Data Erasure**

Data erasure refers to permanently deleting data from a storage device so that it cannot be recovered by any known methods. This process is crucial when disposing of or repurposing appliances to ensure that unauthorised individuals cannot access any sensitive information previously stored on the device.

**Multi-Factor Authentication (MFA)**

Multi-factor authentication (MFA) is a security measure that requires users to provide two or more distinct forms of identification before allowing access to data or systems. This could be a mixture of one time passwords, biometrics, smartcards and more.

# EMPLOYMENT STATUSES

Employment in the UK is defined under various classifications—each category carries specific legal protections and attributes. The three main employment status categories are employees, workers (which includes Limb (b) workers), and self-employed individuals.

In these employment statuses, employees may find it advantageous to join a trade union for additional protection and support. Trade unions can provide advice, guidance, and representation to their members on matters related to employment. They can also negotiate pay, working conditions, and employment rights with employers.

Individuals of all employment statuses in the UK, including 'employees', 'workers (limb b)', and those self-employed, can seek advice from legal professionals or advisory bodies to understand their rights and responsibilities under employment law. Bodies such as Citizen's Advice or the Advisory, Conciliation and Arbitration Service (ACAS) are available to all, regardless of employment status.

**Employee**

An employee in the UK is a person who is engaged under a contract of employment. This contract, spells out the specifics of the employment relationship, delineating the obligations and expectations between the employer and the employee. The contract typically includes details such as work hours, salary, job description, and other conditions of employment.

Employees in the UK enjoy a comprehensive set of rights and protections under employment law. These rights extend to various aspects of their working lives, from leave entitlements to termination procedures. For instance, employees have the right to paid leave, encompassing not just holiday leave but also maternity and paternity leave and sick leave. This ensures employees can take necessary time off without fearing losing their income.

Furthermore, employees are entitled to a minimum notice period before their employment can be terminated, providing them with some level of job security and allowing them time to seek alternative employment. They are also shielded against unfair dismissal, which means that em-

**EMPLOYEE KEY POINTS:**

- They hold a contract of employment.
- They are granted extensive employment rights, including the right to sick pay, holiday pay, parental leave, and flexible working conditions.
- They are protected against unfair dismissal and discrimination.
- If they are made redundant, they are entitled to a redundancy payment.
- They are guaranteed minimum notice periods if their employment is being terminated.
- Their income is subject to PAYE taxation, which the employer deducts.

ployers cannot dismiss them without a valid reason and without following the correct procedure.

Employees also enjoy the right to request flexible working conditions. This could include anything from part-time hours to working from home, and employers are legally obligated to seriously consider—though not obliged to accept—such requests. This right is fundamental in promoting work-life balance and accommodating employees with caring responsibilities or health conditions.

In addition, employees have the right to join or form a trade union, which can provide additional support and representation in the workplace. They are also protected against discrimination based on age, sex, race, disability, religion or belief, sexual orientation, and gender reassignment.

Employees' income is subject to Pay As You Earn (PAYE) taxation. Under this system, the employer must deduct tax and National Insurance contributions from the employee's wages before they are paid. This ensures that the correct amount of tax is paid promptly.

In the UK, employees made redundant are usually entitled to a redundancy payment based on age, length of service, and weekly pay. Generally, this payment is given on their next scheduled payday or shortly after their last day at work. If an employer cannot afford to pay, the employee can seek a direct payment from the Redundancy Payments Service.

**Worker Inc. Limb (b)**

A 'worker' is a broad category that includes traditional employees and others who might not fit the traditional employee mould but still carry out work or services under a contract. This contract can be explicit or implied, oral or in writing. Workers are entitled to certain rights, including receiving at least the National Minimum Wage, statutory minimum paid holiday, rest breaks, protection against unlawful deductions from wages, and protection against discrimination.

On the other hand, a 'limb (b) worker', also known as a 'dependent contractor', is a subcategory of 'worker'. These individuals are typically self-employed but provide service as part of someone else's business. They do not operate as an inde-

**WORKER KEY POINTS:**

- Workers, including Limb (b) workers, maintain a contract or another arrangement to personally provide work or services for a reward.
- They are entitled to employment rights, including National Minimum Wage and protection against unlawful pay deductions.
- They have the right to statutory minimum paid holiday.
- They are entitled to rest breaks and a limit on the maximum working week.
- They can opt out of the 48-hour work week, but it is not a requirement.

pendent business in their own right and are in a subordinate and dependent position relative to their employer.

While limb (b) workers share some of the same rights as traditional workers (like minimum wage and statutory leave), they do not have some of the protections that full employees have. For instance, they do not have the right to claim unfair dismissal or statutory redundancy pay.

The key difference, therefore, lies in the degree of independence and the nature of the relationship with the employer. A limb (b) worker is more integrated into the employer's business and has less independence than a traditional worker who might run their own business. This distinction becomes important in determining the employment rights and protections each category is entitled to under UK employment law.

The distinction between traditional 'workers' and 'limb (b) workers' can be unclear due to the nature of work, autonomy, and contract specifics, a situation further muddled by the gig economy and flexible work arrangements. UK employment law uses tests focused on personal service, control, and whether the individual operates their own business to navigate these complexities, which can significantly impact the rights and protections individuals receive. Thus, employers and workers must comprehend these differences to guarantee everyone is given the appropriate rights and protections under UK employment law.

**Self-Employed**

In the UK, a self-employed individual operates their own business rather than employed by an employer.

This means that they assume full responsibility for the success or failure of their business. They can decide about their work, including when, where, and how they perform it. Furthermore, they can work for multiple clients at any given time. Being self-employed does not grant them the same employment rights as regular employees or workers.

**SELF-EMPLOYED KEY POINTS:**

- Self-employed individuals own businesses and assume full responsibility for their success or failure.
- Unlike employees and workers, self-employed individuals do not have employment rights such as the national minimum wage, paid annual leave, or sick pay.
- Self-employed individuals have the freedom to negotiate their own fees and working conditions with clients.
- They pay their own tax and National Insurance contributions and file annual Self Assessment tax returns.
- They lack certain employment rights, however they are still protected by health and safety laws and anti-discrimination legislation.

For instance, they are not entitled to the national minimum wage, as they are not paid a salary but rather earn income based on the performance of their business. Similarly, they do not have the right to paid annual leave or sick pay, as these are benefits typically provided to employees and workers.

In terms of financial obligations, self-employed individuals are responsible for handling their own tax and National Insurance contributions. They must file a Self Assessment tax return each year, declaring their income and business expenses to HM Revenue and Customs (HMRC). This is a crucial responsibility, as failure to do so can result in penalties. Despite these differences, self-employed individuals also have some form of legal protection. This includes health and safety legislation designed to prevent workplace injuries and illnesses. They are also protected against discrimination based on age, sex, disability, race, religion or sexual orientation under the Equality Act 2010.

In the UK, the self-employed sector is quite diverse, encompassing a wide range of occupations and industries. From freelance professionals and consultants to individuals running their own retail or service-oriented businesses, each self-employed person brings unique skills and offerings. This diversity contributes to the dynamism and innovation in the UK economy, as self-employed individuals often bring new ideas, services, and products to market.

One intriguing aspect of being self-employed in the UK is the opportunity to directly contribute to the local economy. Self-employed individuals often establish businesses catering to their local communities' needs, providing goods and services that might not be otherwise available. This can stimulate local economies, create job opportunities, and foster community development.

Lastly, self-employment in the UK also evolves with global trends and technological advancements. The growth of the digital economy has opened up new opportunities for self-employment. For instance, the gig economy has given rise to many self-employed individuals who offer their skills and services on a project-by-project basis, often remotely.

Similarly, e-commerce platforms have enabled many individuals to start their online businesses. As the business landscape changes, self-employment in the UK will likely evolve, offering new opportunities and challenges for those who choose this career path.

**DID YOU KNOW?**

UK employment law has no specific legal definition for 'self-employed.' This status is typically determined by factors such as control over work and financial risk. While it allows for greater flexibility and control, it does not provide the same legal protection as 'employee' or 'worker' statuses.

# TEST YOURSELF

UK employment law is designed to regulate employers' and employees' rights and obligations. This law encompasses a variety of contract types, including permanent, temporary, and zero-hour contracts. Key areas covered include wages, working hours, holidays, parental leave, and union rights. Additionally, UK employment law incorporates discrimination law, which protects against unfair treatment based on age, gender, race, disability, religion, or sexual orientation. It also enforces workplace health and safety measures and outlines fair dismissal and redundancy procedures. Lastly, this law provides guidelines on handling personal data to ensure employees' privacy is respected and protected.

Furthermore, UK employment law ensures an employer's obligation to provide a safe and secure working environment, which includes measures against workplace bullying and harassment. It also covers regulations regarding the employment of foreign workers, ensuring they have the right to work in the UK and are not exploited. Additionally, the law mandates employers to properly train their employees, ensuring they have the necessary skills and knowledge to perform their tasks safely and effectively.

**COMPARE YOUR ANSWERS**
Example answers to these questions can be found in Appendix IV on Page 190

**1. Under UK employment law, what types of discrimination are prohibited in the workplace?**

..........................................................................................

..........................................................................................

..........................................................................................

..........................................................................................

..........................................................................................

..........................................................................................

..........................................................................................

..........................................................................................

..........................................................................................

..........................................................................................

..........................................................................................

..........................................................................................

**2. What are some of an employer's critical responsibilities regarding Health and Safety in the workplace?**

..........................................................................................

..........................................................................................

..........................................................................................

..........................................................................................

..........................................................................................

..........................................................................................

..........................................................................................

..........................................................................................

..........................................................................................

..........................................................................................

..........................................................................................

..........................................................................................

3. **What is the difference between fair and unfair dismissal under UK employment law?**

4. **How does UK employment law protect employee data?**

**5. What are the different types of employment contracts recognised under UK employment law?**

**6. How does UK employment law define the scope of 'employee' and 'worker'?**

**7. Can UK employers change an employment contract without an employee's consent?**

**8. What rights does an employee have if made redundant in the UK?**

9. **What are the consequences for an employer in failing to adhere to health and safety regulations in the UK?**

10. **How does UK employment law ensure equal pay for men and women?**

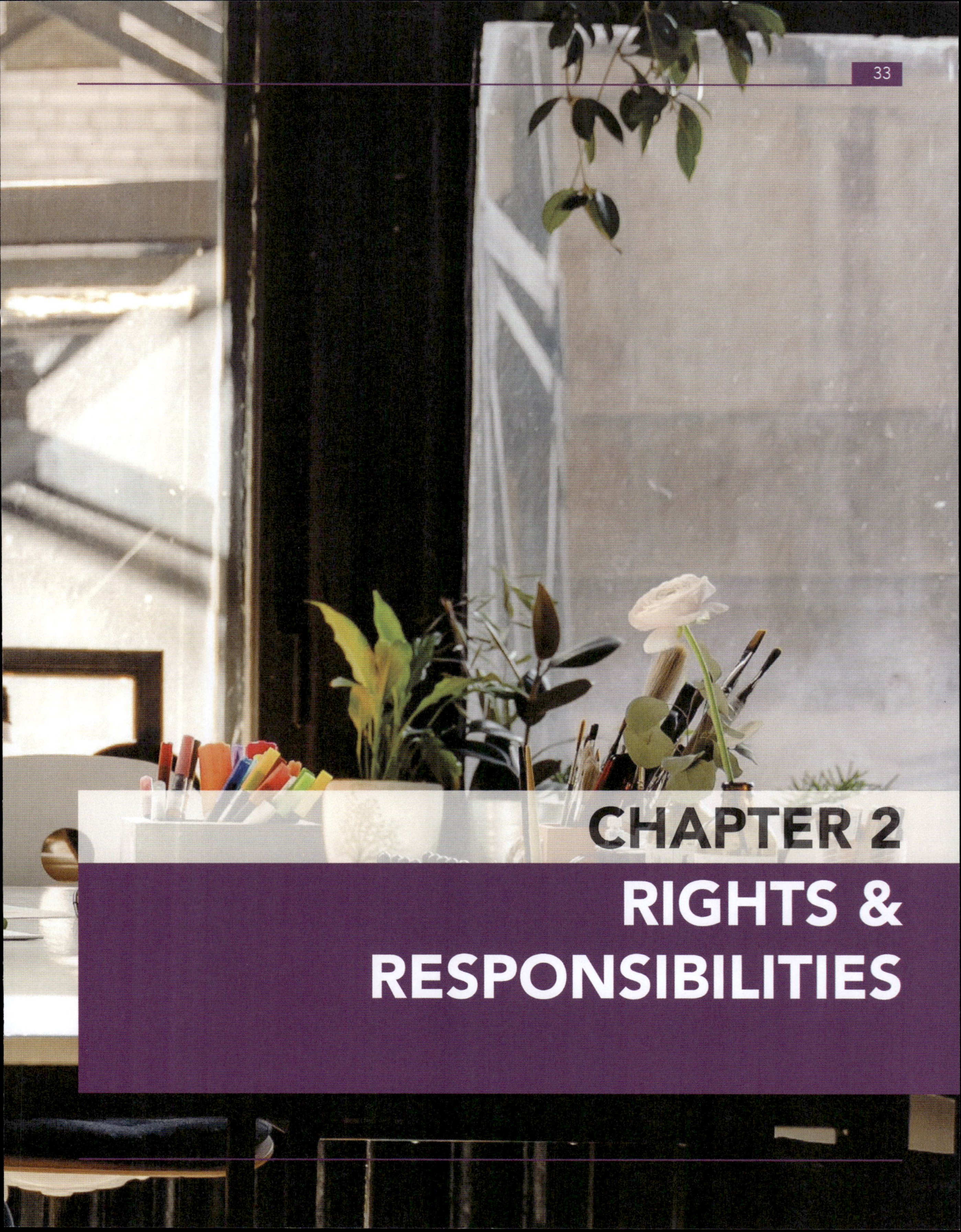

# CHAPTER 2
# RIGHTS & RESPONSIBILITIES

# RIGHTS OF EMPLOYEES

A thorough knowledge of employee rights is critical not only for UK employers but also for their employees. Numerous UK legislations exist to safeguard these rights, each meticulously crafted to promote a balanced, fair, and healthy work environment. While these laws generally apply to all workers, the specifics may vary, influenced by the individual's employment status and personal circumstances.

The National Minimum Wage Act 1998 is a pivotal UK employment law, ensuring a mandated minimum hourly wage for anyone doing work for an employer under contract, the amount of which is dependent on the individual's age and apprenticeship status. This legislation is fundamental to UK employment practices, emphasising fair pay and preventing exploitation. It is regularly reviewed and updated to reflect economic changes.

The Health and Safety at Work etc. Act 1974 is crucial legislation that ensures a safe and hazard-free environment for employees. Employers must secure the health, safety, and welfare of their employees and anyone impacted by their operations, which might involve providing essential safety equipment or offering safety training to mitigate work-related risks. This applies universally, disregarding the worker's employment status.

Protection against unfair dismissal falls under the Employment Rights Act 1996. Unfair dismissal is when an employer terminates an employee's contract violating UK employment laws. This could occur due to discrimination, whistleblowing, or dismissal without a valid reason or due process. However, this right is primarily reserved for 'employees' and may not extend to 'workers' or the self-employed.

Despite the lack of protection for 'workers' and the self-employed, there are still some circumstances under which they might have recourse. For instance, if they prove that their dismissal resulted from discriminatory practices, they can bring a claim under the Equality Act 2010. If they can demonstrate that they were dismissed due to whistleblowing, they may be protected under the Public Interest Disclosure Act 1998.

**LEGAL CONVERGEANCE**

The UK's Employment Rights Act 1996 brought together critical elements from several previous acts and introduced new ones. These predecessors include the Contracts of Employment Act 1963, which first mandated written employment contracts, and the Redundancy Payments Act 1965, which established redundancy rights. The ERA further built on the Employment Protection Act 1975's maternity rights provisions. These landmark legislations were absorbed and enhanced by the ERA 1996, allowing it to more comprehensively address the evolving needs and rights of employees in the UK.

# TIMELINE OF KEY 'EMPLOYEE' RIGHTS

**1974**

**Health & Safety at Work Act (1974)**
Right to a healthy and safe workplace

**1982**

**Statutory Sick Pay (General) Regs. (1982)**
Right to paid sick leave

**1996**

**Employment Rights Act (1996)**
Right to receive written employment particulars
Right to an itemised payslip
Protection against unfair deductions from wages
Increased rights around health & safety
Right to time off for public & trade union duties
Protection against unfair dismissal

**1998**

**National Minimum Wage Act (1998)**
Right to earn at least the National Minimum Wage

**Working Time Regulations (1998)**
Right to a minimum number of days paid leave

**1999**

**Maternity & Parental Leave etc Regs. (1999)**
Right to take maternity / parental leave

**2000**

**Part-time Workers (P.L.F.T) Regulations (2000)**
Equal rights for part-time workers

**2002**

**Fixed-term Workers (P.L.F.T) Regulations (2002)**
Equal rights for fixed-term employees

**2004**

**Information & Consultation of Employees Regs. (2004)**
Right to be informed & consulted on specific company issues

**2006**

**Work & Families Act (2006)**
Extended rights for maternity, adoption, and carers

**2010**

**Equality Act (2010)**
Right to a discrimination free work environment

**Agency Workers Regulations (2010)**
Same employment & working conditions for agency workers after a 12-week qualifying period

**2014**

**Flexible Working Regs. (2014)**
Right to request flexible working hours

**2015**

**Modern Slavery Act (2015)**
Protection against slavery and human trafficking

# TIMELINE OF KEY WORKER / LIMB (B) RIGHTS

The Working Time Regulations 1998 regulate the maximum number of hours an employee can work in a week and also offers the right to rest breaks, daily rest, and annual leave. The law stipulates that an adult worker should not exceed an average of 48 hours a week—a calculation made over 17 weeks. This law applies to most workers and employees, exempting those self-employed or running businesses.

The Employment Act 2002 provides 'employees' the right to request flexible working arrangements after a qualifying period of employment, currently set at 26 weeks. This law does not extend to 'workers' or self-employed individuals.

In addition to these fundamental rights, UK law also grants employees benefits such as maternity leave, paternity leave, and protection against discrimination. However, these rights can fluctuate based on the employment status—employee, worker, or self-employed—and the individual circumstances of the worker.

The 2020 Supreme Court verdict in the Uber BV v Aslam & Others case expanded 'worker' rights by classifying Uber drivers as 'limb (b) workers,' who are contracted for personal services but not part of the employer's profession. This granted them rights, including minimum wage, paid leave, rest breaks, and protections against discrimination and whistleblowing, but not the right to unfair dismissal, redundancy payments, or flexible working requests.

## 1974

**Health & Safety at Work Act (1974)**
Right to a healthy and safe workplace

## 1992

**Trade Union & Labour Relations (Cons.) Act (1992)**
Right to belong to a trade union
Protection against dismissal for trade union activities

## 1996

**Employment Rights Act (1996)**
Protection against unfair deductions from pay

## 1998

**National Minimum Wage Act (1998)**
Right to earn at least National Minimum Wage
**Public Interest Disclosure Act (1998)**
Protection for 'whistleblowing'
**Working Time Regulations (1998)**
Right to a limit on working time

## 1999

**Maternity and Parental Leave, etc Regs (1999)**
Right to take maternity / parental leave

## 2002

**Employment Rights Act (2002)**
Right to a statutory redundancy payment

## 2008

**Pensions Act (2008)**
Right to automatic enrolment in a workplace pension

## 2010

**Equality Act (2010)**
Right to a discrimination free workplace
**Agency Workers Regulations (2010)**
Right to equal working conditions as employees after 12 weeks

## 2018

**Data Protection Act (2018)**
Right to a control over personal data

# TIMELINE OF KEY 'SELF-EMPLOYED' RIGHTS

**1974**

**Health & Safety at Work Act (1974)**
Right to a healthy and safe workplace

**1996**

**Employment Rights Act (1996)**
Further rights to a healthy and safe workplace
Potential protection around discrimination
Some data protection rights
Some protection around 'whistleblowing'

**1998**

**Public Interest Disclosure Act (1998)**
Further protection for 'whistleblowing'

**2003**

**Income Tax (Earnings & Pensions) Act**
Rights around taxation

**2008**

**Pensions Act (2008)**
Right to opt-in to workplace pension

**2010**

**Agency Workers Regulations (2010)**
Equal work conditions for some freelancers / contractors

**2018**

**Data Protection Act (2018)**
Right to a control over personal data

In the UK, there is a significant contrast between the protections granted to 'limb (b) workers', also known as 'dependent contractors', and those who are self-employed. Limb (b) workers are individuals who, while not employees, offer their services as components of another's business. They are entitled to an array of employment rights.

Contrarily, self-employed individuals operate their own businesses and lack the degree of protection enjoyed by employees or limb (b) workers. Although they possess greater freedom over their work, they also shoulder more risk and responsibility. Self-employed individuals do not receive employment benefits such as minimum wage, paid holiday, or protection against discrimination from the businesses they contract with. They are solely responsible for their own tax and National Insurance contributions. They must register with HM Revenue and Customs (HMRC) for Self Assessment.

Self-employment provides unique benefits, including control over work-life balance, business decisions, the potential for direct influence on income, and eligibility for certain tax deductions. Yet, it demands increased responsibility and self-discipline to ensure business success. Regarding protections, the Equality Act 2010 protects self-employed individuals contracted for personal work against discrimination, but those working under a company name or who can delegate may lack coverage. Thus, while advantageous, self-employment presents its complexities and challenges.

# RIGHT OF ACCESS

The 'Right of Access' is an essential element of UK employment law, falling under the broader scope of data protection principles. While the General Data Protection Regulation (GDPR) is a European Union regulation, the UK has incorporated aspects into its own Data Protection Act 2018 following its exit from the EU.

The 'Right of Access' under the GDPR gives individuals, or 'data subjects', the ability to access personal data that an organisation, like an employer, has stored. This is often known as a Subject Access Request (SAR).

When an employer receives a SAR, they must provide the following details:

1. A copy of the data held on the subject. The types of personal data involved could include the individual's name, contact information, and work history.

2. The reasons for processing the data: This explains why the employer needs to use the individual's data.

3. Who the personal data has been or will be shared with. This could be other company sections or outside companies such as those providing payroll services.

4. The expected storage duration for the personal data or the factors used to decide this duration.

Employers must respond to a SAR without undue delay and generally within one month of receipt of the request. This period can be extended for two months, considering the complexity and number of requests.

Employers are not permitted to impose a fee for the service unless a 'Subject Access Request' (SAR) is deemed 'manifestly unfounded or excessive'. If an employer decides to deny a SAR, they must provide a reason for refusing the individual. Additionally, they must inform the individual of their right to complain to a relevant supervisory authority. In the context of the UK, the appropriate authority would be the Information Commissioner's Office (ICO). They should also inform the individual about their right to seek a judicial remedy.

The 'Right of Access' is critical to maintaining a fair and transparent workplace. It ensures that employees can monitor and manage how their personal information is used, contributing to a more open and trustful employer-employee relationship.

In our digital era, the 'Right of Access' principle under the UK's Data Protection Act 2018 underscores the importance of proper data handling. More than just a legal obligation, it is a trust-building tool. Employers are urged to respond to SARs, implement comprehensive data management policies, conduct regular audits, and consider appointing a dedicated Data Protection Officer (DPO).

# RIGHT TO ERASURE

The 'Right to Erasure', also known as the 'Right to be Forgotten', is a principle that initially originated from the General Data Protection Regulation (GDPR) implemented by the European Union. This regulation empowers individuals to request the deletion of their data from an organisation's records if they no longer want it to be processed.

In the context of UK employment law, the 'Right to Erasure' empowers employees, workers, contractors, and job applicants to request the deletion or removal of personal data held by their current, past, or potential employers unless there is a compelling reason for its continued processing. This right is not absolute and applies only in certain circumstances. For instance, employers might not be required to erase the data if it is necessary to comply with a legal obligation or to perform a contract. When an erasure request is received, employers must respond preferably within one month. If the request is complex or multiple requests, this period can be extended by two months. Non-compliance with these provisions can lead to significant penalties imposed by the Information Commissioner's Office (ICO), the UK's independent authority set up to uphold information rights.

Failure to comply with the 'Right to Erasure' can have severe repercussions for businesses, with the Information Commissioner's Office (ICO) authorised to impose hefty fines of up to €20 million or 4% of the organisation's global annual turnover. Non-compliance can also harm a company's reputation, potentially leading to a loss of trust among employees, contractors, and prospective job applicants and potentially affecting the quality of applicants or talent retention. Additionally, the ICO may order businesses to cease data processing, significantly disrupting operations.

Extending the discussion around the 'Right to Erasure', it is essential to note that individuals must provide valid grounds for erasure. These could include situations where their data is no longer necessary for the initially collected purpose, when they withdraw consent, or when they object to the processing.

The 'Right to Erasure' is crucial in managing public information, especially in the digital age. This right is particularly relevant when it comes to information society services that are accessible to children. In the era of digital information, data about individuals, including children, can become widely disseminated across numerous platforms, often in the public domain.

Lastly, while the 'Right to Erasure' is a powerful tool for individuals, it is also an obligation that organisations must manage carefully. For businesses, this means implementing clear data-handling policies and training employees to handle such requests appropriately. Companies must establish effective mechanisms to identify, assess and act upon erasure requests, as failure to do so could lead to penalties enforced by the ICO. This underlines the significance of the 'Right to Erasure' in fostering a culture of respect for privacy rights in UK employment law.

# TRANSFER OF UNDERTAKINGS PROTECTION

Specific rules and regulations emerge when a business or a portion of it in the UK changes ownership. These are outlined in the Transfer of Undertakings (Protection of Employment) Regulations 2006 (TUPE).

**Preservation of Employment Contracts**
As per Regulation 4 of the TUPE Regulations, the employees' contracts are automatically transferred to the new employer, maintaining the same terms and conditions.

**Protection Against Dismissal**
Regulation 7 of the TUPE Regulations provides protection against unfair dismissal. If an employee is dismissed because of the transfer or a reason connected with it that is not an economic, technical, or organisational reason, the dismissal is automatically unfair.

**Informing & Consulting Employees**
Regulations 13-15 of the TUPE Regulations outline the requirements for the employer to inform and consult recognised trade unions or elected employee representatives about the transfer.

**Pension Rights**
Regulation 10 of the TUPE Regulations states that the new employer is not obligated to maintain the employees' existing pension rights.

**Liability for Failure to Inform & Consult**
Regulation 15 of the TUPE Regulations states that employees may claim to a tribunal if the employer fails to inform or consult appropriately.

Under TUPE, it is worth mentioning that a change in service provision can also trigger these regulations. For example, if a company decides to outsource a function of its business, bring a previously outsourced function in-house, or change the contractor providing a service, these situations could also fall under TUPE. In such cases, employees fundamentally attached to the function being transferred might have their contracts transferred to the new service provider. Also, an essential aspect of TUPE involves requiring the outgoing employer (transferor) to provide the incoming employer (transferee) with specific information about the transferring employees. This is known as Employee Liability Information and includes details such as the identities of the employees, their employment terms, and any disciplinary or grievance records. The transferor is legally required to provide this information at least 28 days before the transfer occurs.

While TUPE aims to protect employees during business transfers, there are circumstances where employers can lawfully change the terms of employment post-transfer if they have an Economic, Technical, or Organisational (ETO) reason entailing changes in the workforce.

Other regulations, such as the Employment Rights Act 1996, the Trade Union and Labour Relations (Consolidation) Act 1992, and the Pensions Act 2004, may also apply depending on the situation's specifics. This is a complex area and often requires legal advice to ensure compliance with the regulations.

# NATIONAL INSURANCE

National Insurance (NI) is a fundamental aspect of UK employment law. It was established under the National Insurance Act 1911 and represents a system of taxes paid by workers and employers in the UK, contributing to various state benefits.

**Classification of NI Contributions (NICs):**
Both employees and employers pay NICs, categorised into different 'classes'. Class 1 NICs are paid by employees and employers, with the contribution amount based on the employee's earnings and their respective 'band'.

**Role in Employee Benefits**
The amount of NICs an employee pays influences eligibility for benefits, including the State Pension, Jobseeker's Allowance, Employment and Support Allowance, and Maternity Allowance.

**Employer's Responsibility**
Employers must deduct Class 1 contributions from wages through the PAYE (Pay As You Earn) system. Non-compliance can lead to financial penalties from HM Revenue and Customs..

**Self-Employed Individuals**
Class 2 and Class 4 NICs apply for those self-employed, depending on their profits. These contributions also contribute towards certain benefits.

**Exceptions & Rebates**
Different rules may apply to specific categories of workers, such as mariners. Some may be entitled to a National Insurance rebate, such as individuals enrolled in contracted-out pension schemes.

**Reporting & Record Keeping**
Employers must maintain detailed records of the NICs they have deducted and report details to HMRC. Penalties can ensue for non-compliance.

**Updates & Changes**
The UK government periodically updates NI rates and categories. Therefore, both employees and employers must stay updated of these changes.

The alterations in these rates and categories could significantly impact the levels of contributions from both parties. It is essential to regularly check official government websites to ensure compliance with the most recent NI regulations.

**DID YOU KNOW?**
Your National Insurance number, a unique set of letters and numbers, is your identifier within the UK's tax system throughout your life. This number is crucial for tax purposes, accessing the healthcare system and receiving benefits.

Regardless of any life changes, such as moving abroad, changing your name due to marriage or becoming self-employed, your National Insurance number remains consistent, ensuring your contributions and benefits are accurately recorded. It is like your financial fingerprint in the UK, making it an essential part of your work and social security records.

# RESPONSIBILITIES OF EMPLOYERS

In the UK, employers are bound by a complex network of legal obligations designed to protect the rights and welfare of their employees. Each law and regulation has been crafted to address distinct aspects of employment, making the workplace a just, safe, and dignified environment.

**Promise of Fair Payment**

The National Minimum Wage Act 1998 ensures that every pound earned is deserved. This Act mandates employers to pay their employees a minimum wage, as the UK government specifies. This legal requirement ensures that employees who work full-time, part-time, or on a contractual basis receive a salary commensurate with their efforts. It is not just about financial stability but about fostering a sense of fairness and equality in the workplace.

**Privacy & Dignity**

The Human Rights Act 1998 and the Data Protection Act 2018 act as the guardians of employees' privacy and dignity. These laws ordain employers to protect personal data and refrain from any behaviour that may be intrusive or degrading. These principles are sacrosanct, applying to all employees, regardless of rank or role, ensuring a respectful and dignified workplace. Furthermore, these legislations impose an onus on companies to adopt robust measures safeguarding employee data and maintaining confidentiality. They also promote mutual respect and courtesy, fostering an environment where everyone can thrive professionally without fear of unwarranted intrusions or disrespect.

**Creating a Safe Environment**

The Health and Safety at Work etc. Act 1974 establishes the workplace as a safe sanctuary. This Act implores employers to provide a healthy working environment, including implementing necessary safety measures, offering sufficient health and safety training, and ensuring all machinery and equipment are safe and fit. It is about reducing accidents and promoting overall well-being and peace of mind in the workforce.

**Fair Disciplinary & Greivance**

The ACAS (Advisory, Conciliation and Arbitration Service) Code of Practice on Disciplinary and Grievance Procedures serves as a roadmap to navigate the complex labyrinth of disciplinary and grievance issues in the workplace. Employers must ensure these procedures are conducted fairly and reasonably, respecting the rights of all employees, regardless of their employment status.

**Fair Employment Contracts**

The Employment Rights Act 1996 is a cornerstone of fair employment contracts. This Act necessitates that all employment contracts be transparent, clear, and equitable. This implies that the terms and conditions of employment should be clearly defined and comprehensive to the employee, irrespective of the nature of their employment contract. It is more than fine print—it promotes transparency and fosters mutual understanding between the employer and employee.

**Equality**

The Equality Act 2010 is a pivotal piece of UK legislation designed to protect employees from workplace discrimination. This act is not just about preventing discrimination; it promotes an environment of fairness, equality, and respect. This includes nine protected characteristics: age, disability, gender reassignment, marriage and civil partnership, pregnancy and maternity, race, religion or belief, sex, and sexual orientation.

Non-compliance with the responsibilities outlined in this legislation can lead to severe consequences for employers. These repercussions can be financial penalties determined by Employment Tribunals. The severity of these penalties varies, depending on the nature and extent of the discrimination. This underscores the crucial importance for businesses to fulfil these fundamental legal obligations and maintain a harmonious workplace. However, this overview is quite general, and each area can be complex. Employers may also have additional responsibilities under other laws and regulations, depending on the specifics of their business and employees. Therefore, it is always advisable for employers to seek legal advice to ensure they are fully compliant with all relevant laws and regulations.

The Equality Act 2010 also requires employers to make reasonable adjustments for employees with disabilities. This may include altering physical aspects of the workplace, changing working hours, or providing extra support for disabled employees. Employers must consider each case individually and make necessary modifications to avoid disadvantages. Failure to do so could be seen as discrimination, leading to potential legal proceedings. The definition of 'reasonable' can be subjective, so employers must seek legal advice to meet this requirement.

In the broader context of equality, employers must also be aware of their responsibilities concerning equal pay. The Equality Act 2010 stipulates that men and women must receive equal compensation for similar work. This extends to all terms and conditions in the employment contract, not just basic pay. It covers holiday entitlement, pension benefits, company cars, and bonus schemes. Employers must conduct regular pay audits to ensure compliance with these regulations. Employees who feel they are not receiving equal pay have the right to request information from their employer to establish whether there is a discrepancy and why.

Furthermore, the act also covers indirect discrimination, which occurs when a company's policies, practices or procedures disadvantage people of a particular group. For example, requiring all employees to work full-time could indirectly discriminate against women, as statistics show they are more likely to work part-time due to childcare responsibilities. Employers must ensure their policies are fair and not unintentionally disadvantage certain groups. If indirect discrimination is found, the employer must be able to justify the policy by showing it is a proportionate means of achieving a legitimate aim.

# IMPERATIVE OF EQUALITY

Central to the ethos of UK employment law is an unwavering principle: the persistent dedication to nurturing equality and eradicating discrimination in the workplace. This commitment is not merely a moral obligation but a legal imperative rigorously enforced through key legislative frameworks like the Equality Act 2010.

The Equality Act 2010 is a paramount legislative platform that categorically prohibits discrimination, harassment, and victimisation based on nine unique 'protected characteristics'. These incorporate age, disability, gender reassignment, marriage and civil partnership status, pregnancy and maternity conditions, race, religion or belief, sex, and sexual orientation. This Act ensures that all employees, regardless of this individual characteristic, are granted equal treatment and impartiality in the workplace.

In addition to the Equality Act 2010, other impactful legislation, such as the Employment Rights Act 1996 and the Human Rights Act 1998, also play a critical role in shielding employees from discrimination and unjust treatment in the workplace. Employers carry a legal onus to foster a diverse and inclusive work environment.

This responsibility extends to making 'reasonable adjustments' for employees with disabilities. This may involve modifying work schedules, providing specific equipment, or reconfiguring tasks to enable these employees to perform their duties proficiently.

Moreover, employers must accommodate their employees' diverse needs and rights where feasible. This could entail observing religious holidays, offering appropriate maternity or paternity leave, or ensuring equal opportunities for employees undergoing gender reassignment. However, the specific actions required can vary based on the individual circumstances and the nature of the job, and there may be exceptions in some instances.

These principles of equality and non-discrimination are universally applicable, regardless of employment status. Whether employees are full-time, part-time, temporary, or contract-based, they are all entitled to the same degree of respect and fairness under the law.

In essence, UK law underscores the undeniable importance of promoting equality and abolishing discrimination in the workplace. However, the successful implementation and enforcement of these principles can depend on various factors, including the awareness and understanding of these laws by employers and employees, the effectiveness of organisational policies and procedures, and the availability of resources to handle complaints and disputes.

This commitment is not only vital for maintaining a harmonious and productive work environment, but it is also a legal mandate that employers are required to adhere to.

UK law advocates for transparent, fair recruitment. All potential employees must receive equal opportunity via transparent job descriptions and consistent selection criteria. Unconscious bias could breach the Equality Act 2010. Therefore, regular training sessions are encouraged for employers and employees.

**DID YOU KNOW?**
The Equality Act of 2010 established the 'public sector equality duty', obligating public institutions such as local authorities or government departments to prevent discrimination and foster equality. These institutions must examine how their decisions can alleviate disadvantages experienced by individuals with protected characteristics.

Additionally, the law supports work-life balance via flexible working rights. Employees with 26 weeks of employment can legally request flexible working arrangements. This accommodates diverse needs, potentially enhancing productivity. Employers, however, can refuse such requests with valid business reasons as long as they comply with the Equality Act 2010. This reflects societal recognition of work-life balance.

# TEST YOURSELF

UK employment law provides a suite of protections and responsibilities for employees and employers. Employees have certain rights, including the Right of Access and the Right to Erasure, which pertain to their ability to access personal data held by their employer and request its deletion, respectively. Further, the Transfer of Undertakings Protection of Employment (TUPE) provides safeguards when a business is transferred or services are outsourced, including the protection of employees' terms and conditions of employment.

On the other hand, employers have responsibilities, including ensuring a safe and healthy workplace, providing written employment agreements, and paying employees fairly and regularly. Lastly, the imperative of equality is a fundamental principle underpinning UK employment law, requiring employers to treat all employees fairly and without discrimination, promoting a culture of inclusivity and respect in the workplace.

**COMPARE YOUR ANSWERS**

Example answers to these questions can be found in Appendix IV on Page 192

1. **What fundamental rights are every employee entitled to?**

2. **What does "Right of Access" mean in the employment law context?**

3. **What is the "Right to Erasure" in the employment law context?**

4. **What are some key responsibilities of employers?**

**5. In the employment law context, what is the "Imperative of Equality"?**

**6. What is the process for an employee to raise a grievance?**

**7. What are the exceptions to the 'Right to Erasure'?**

**8. What responsibilities do employers have regarding employee training?**

9. **How does TUPE protect employee rights during a business transfer?**

10. **How can employers demonstrate commitment to the "Imperative of Equality?"**

Controller (for Capex items)
For any item not budgeted
for the purchase.
Signature 4:
Signature 4:

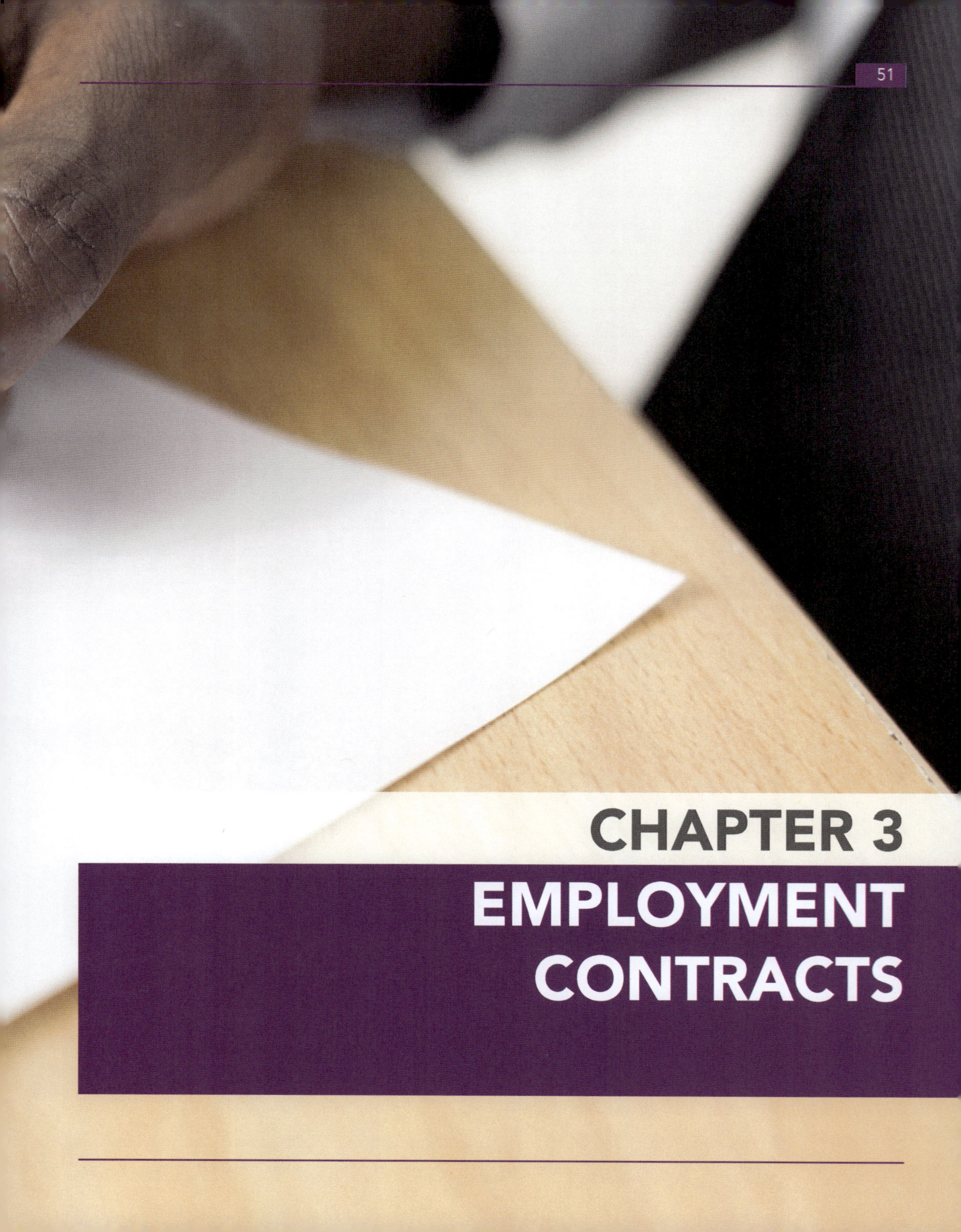

# CHAPTER 3
# EMPLOYMENT CONTRACTS

# DEFINITION & SIGNIFICANCE

In its most rudimentary form, an employment contract is a legally binding agreement that outlines and establishes the conditions of the professional rapport between an employer and an employee.

This crucial document meticulously delineates both parties' rights, duties, and obligations, serving as a comprehensive manual for their professional interaction.

Imagine an employment contract as the blueprint of your job role. It delineates the expectations your employer has for you, your anticipations from your employer, and the repercussions if these expectations are not met. It operates as a protective shield, laying the groundwork for a synergistic and productive work atmosphere.

In the realm of UK employment law, employment contracts play a pivotal role. They work as a compass, steering employers and employees through the complex maze of workplace guidelines and expectations. These contracts safeguard both parties, facilitating a balanced and transparent professional relationship.

Numerous critical UK laws supervise the creation and implementation of employment contracts. The Employment Rights Act 1996 is one such law that mandates a primary statement on the first day of employment and detailed written information containing specific details within the first two months. Information such as the employee's remuneration, working hours, holiday allowances, and notice periods ought to be explicitly mentioned in the contract.

Moreover, the Equality Act 2010, another significant law in the UK, forbids any form of unjust treatment or discrimination in the workplace based on parameters such as age, race, gender, religion, and disability. Consequently, the employment contract should be in harmony with these laws, protecting the legal rights of both parties involved.

**DID YOU KNOW?**
In the UK, the Working Time Regulations 1998 generally limits the average working week to 48 hours, typically measured over a 17-week reference period. However, workers aged 18 or over can voluntarily work more than this limit by signing a '48-hour opt-out agreement'.

The worker can cancel this agreement at any time, with a standard notice period of a week. However, a more extended notice period may be mutually agreed upon (up to a maximum of three months).

Even with this opt-out, employers are legally bound by the Health and Safety at Work Act 1974 to ensure their employees' health, safety, and welfare. This includes preventing excessively long working hours that could negatively impact an employee.

It is also crucial to comprehend that UK law acknowledges different classifications of 'employment status'—employee, worker, and self-employed, each with distinct rights and obligations.

An 'employee' is entitled to more employment rights and responsibilities than a 'worker', while a 'self-employed' individual has fewer legal employment rights but enjoys greater flexibility. For instance, an 'employee' is often entitled to benefits like sick leave and vacation time, a 'worker' may only be guaranteed the minimum wage, and a 'self-employed' individual can choose their work hours and clients.

Understanding an employment contract goes beyond knowing your role. It encompasses understanding your rights and responsibilities, the legal recourse available to you in the workplace, and the legal framework that supports your employment status. A contract extends beyond recorded or verbalised agreements. It encompasses implied terms, which can considerably alter the contract's stipulations despite not being explicitly stated. These terms may derive from an employer or an employee's actions or conduct, standard practices in the workplace, or even job necessities for effective performance. For example, if an employee has been receiving a company car consistently over the years, this practice could form an implied contract term, irrespective of its documentation. This illustrates the fluidity of employment contracts, which can progress and transform based on actions and routine practices, as opposed to being static, inflexible documents.

# KEY ELEMENTS OF A CONTRACT

In the UK, an employment contract must contain certain fundamental elements to be considered valid. These crucial components, mandated by the Employment Rights Act 1996, safeguard the interests of both the employer and the employee.

They ensure that the conditions of employment are clearly articulated, transparent, and easily understandable to all parties involved.

**Identification of Parties**

It is crucial for the contract to accurately specify the names of both the employer and the employee. This specification is fundamental in designating who is legally obligated to adhere to the contractual terms.

**Commencement Date & Job Description**

The contract must specify the commencement date of employment, as this date will determine the length of service, which may impact entitlements such as redundancy payments and the right to claim for unfair dismissal. Moreover, the contract should specify the job title or describe the role's duties and responsibilities. This ensures a mutual understanding of expectations between employer and employee and may prevent disputes over work expectations.

Effective 6 April 2020, all workers, not just employees, have the right to receive a written statement of particulars of employment on or before the first day of their work. This also aids in preventing any potential disputes arising from ambiguity in the contract.

**Compensation & Working Hours**

The employment contract should clearly define the employee's pay, the method used to calculate it, and the payment frequency. It is also required to outline the typical working hours, including any expectations for weekend, night, or overtime work. This is essential to clarify the employee's work expectations and the corresponding remuneration they will receive.

**Workplace Location**

The contract should clearly state the primary workplace location for employees. If multiple locations or potential relocations are involved in the role, these should be included in the contract to avoid miscommunication or disputes. The legal necessity for this depends on the job's specifics. Changes to the workplace post-contract usually need the employee's agreement unless a mobility clause permits such alterations. However, employers should manage such changes reasonably.

**Holiday Entitlement**

The contract should specify the employee's holiday allowance. The UK law requires a minimum of 5.6 weeks of paid annual leave, including bank holidays. Part-time employees get less, based on their work days. For example, someone working three days a week is entitled to a minimum of 16.8 paid leave days. The contract may provide extra time off beyond the minimum. These specifics in the contract inform the employee of their rest rights and how their work schedule impacts it

**Termination Notice Period**

The contract should specify the notice period required for termination by either party. This period can vary, but it must meet minimum legal requirements. This clarity helps prevent sudden stops and gives both parties time to plan for the change.

**Sick Pay & Pension Schemes**

The contract should include details about sick pay arrangements beyond the Statutory Sick Pay (SSP) that the company offers and information about its pension scheme if it exists. This information is crucial for employees to effectively plan for unexpected circumstances such as sickness and long-term retirement planning. In the UK, it is a legal requirement for employers to provide this information to their employees.

**Confidentiality & Non-Compete Clauses**

Some employment contracts may include clauses related to confidentiality and non-competition. Confidentiality clauses prevent employees from disclosing sensitive company information during and after employment. Non-compete clauses restrict employees from engaging in similar jobs within a certain period after leaving the company. These clauses protect the company's interests but must be reasonable in scope and duration and not unduly restrict the employee's prospects.

**Grievance Procedures**

While it is not a legal requirement to include the grievance procedure in the employment contract, all employers must have a known and accessible grievance procedure in line with the ACAS Code of Practice. This procedure provides a structured process to resolve concerns or complaints during employment.

**Employment Status**

The contract should comprehensively outline the worker's employment status, whether full-time, part-time, temporary, or a zero-hours contract, due to its impact on employment rights, tax obligations, and pension contributions.

**Collective Agreements**

If collective agreements affect an employee's terms and conditions, these should be stated in the employment contract. Collective agreements can be between an employer and a trade union or staff association. The specifics can vary, and employers and employees are strongly advised to seek legal counsel when dealing with employment contracts and collective agreements.

**Changes to the Contract**

The contract should also specify how changes to the agreement can be made. Any changes usually require the understanding of both the employer and the employee. In some cases, specific changes may require the employee's express consent.

Remember, it is not just about having the contract in place but ensuring that it is fair and reasonable for all parties involved. The employer and the employee have rights and responsibilities that should be respected and adhered to.

# CONTRACTUAL RIGHTS

In the UK, employment law bestows specific rights to employees and employers. These are not just mere recommendations or guidelines—they are legal obligations entrenched in several UK laws and statutes, adhering to which is not optional. Employees have a series of fundamental rights. To begin with, their safety at work is non-negotiable—the Health and Safety at Work etc. Act 1974 obliges employers to ensure a secure and hazard-free work environment. Additionally, employees have the right to fair compensation for their labour, which is to be paid timely, according to the Employment Rights Act 1996.

Moreover, employees have the right to adequate rest periods, maternity and paternity leave, sick leave, and other forms of respite under the Working Time Regulations 1998. The laudable Equality Act 2010 protects employees from discrimination based on gender, race, disability, religion, or sexual orientation. Furthermore, employees are free to join a trade union of their preference. They are safeguarded against unjust dismissal, as encapsulated in the Trade Union and Labour Relations (Consolidation) Act 1992 and the Employment Rights Act 1996, respectively.

Employers, on the other hand, also possess a suite of rights. They have the right to expect their employees to deliver their duties to a reasonable standard and uphold professional and responsible conduct in the workplace. Employers have the authority to manage and operate their businesses as they deem fit, on the condition that they respect their employees' rights and abide by all pertinent laws.

While legally binding, an employment contract also serves as a crucial compass for understanding and navigating the complex topography of UK employment law. It outlines a clear path for employees and employers to understand their rights and obligations. Both parties must thoroughly read and comprehend the terms of this contract before establishing an employment agreement to foster a harmonious and lawful working relationship. However, the labyrinth of employment rights can be intricate and additional rights and regulations are potentially applicable based on specific circumstances. For instance, various provisions might exist for part-time or temporary workers or those in particular industries. Thus, when uncertainties or issues arise, it is prudent to seek professional legal advice.

**DID YOU KNOW?**
In the UK, employees have the right to 'time off for dependants'. This allows employees to take time off to deal with emergencies involving a dependant. It is usually a day or two and is typically unpaid. Still, it is available from the first day of employment, regardless of service length.

Under UK employment law, an employee's rights and obligations are not limited to what is expressly stated in the employment contract. The implied terms of an employment contract play a vital part in regulating the employee-employer relationship. These are duties and rights not explicitly mentioned in the contract but are understood to exist. One of these implied terms is the duty of mutual trust and confidence, necessitating both parties not to behave in a manner that would harm or destroy their relationship. An example could be an employer not unjustly criticising an employee's work or an employee not divulging sensitive company information.

Another critical aspect of employment contracts is the right to privacy. Despite being in an employment relationship, employees still enjoy a reasonable expectation of privacy. The Data Protection Act 2018 and the General Data Protection Regulation (GDPR) provide employees with various rights concerning their data, including the right to access data their employer holds about them and correct inaccurate information. Employers must be cautious in collecting, using, and storing their employees' data, ensuring they respect their privacy rights. Finally, the right to be informed about changes in the employment contract is pivotal. According to the Employment Rights Act 1996, employers are obliged to provide their employees with a written statement of changes if any amendment is made to the terms of their employment contract. This ensures transparency and clarity, enabling employees to understand their current position.

# INDUSTRY SPECIFIC RIGHTS

Industry specific rights in the UK refer to certain regulations and standards uniquely applicable to different sectors or industries. These rights are established and governed by a variety of sources. Legislation passed by the UK Parliament, such as the Health and Safety at Work Act 1974 and the Working Time Regulations 1998, forms a significant part of these rights. These laws lay the groundwork for employers' and employees' rights and duties.

Regulatory bodies specific to certain industries also play a crucial role in creating these rights. For instance, the Financial Conduct Authority (FCA) sets regulations for the UK's financial services industry. At the same time, the Health and Safety Executive (HSE) provides comprehensive guidelines for workplace safety across various industries.

Despite the UK's departure from the European Union, many rights previously established under EU law continue to be part of UK law under the European Union (Withdrawal) Act 2018. These include protections relating to working time, discrimination, and health and safety.

Trade unions also contribute to these rights in industries where they have a significant presence through negotiations for their members. Additionally, case law, derived from court decisions, contributes to the creation and interpretation of these rights, particularly where there is ambiguity in legislation or new situations that have yet to be covered by existing laws.

Employers must adhere to these rights and regulations, ensuring a safe and fair work environment. On the other hand, employees should be aware of these rights to safeguard their interests and secure proper treatment. Both parties must maintain a mutual understanding and respect for these rights to foster a cooperative and effective workplace.

Though these 'Industry Specific Rights' play a significant role in dictating the terms of employment, they are not typically included in an employment contract. An employment contract contains terms specific to the position and the company, not industry-wide regulations. These rights are dynamic and subject to changes and updates prompted by new legislation, technological advances, shifts in industry practices, or other relevant factors. Therefore, employers and employees must stay informed and updated about these 'Industry Specific Rights' to ensure compliance and promote a fair and balanced work environment.

**Construction Industry**

In the construction industry, there are specific health and safety regulations, notably the Construction (Design and Management) Regulations 2015. Furthermore, the industry has a distinct taxation scheme known as the Construction Industry Scheme (CIS), and there are regulations concerning self-employment status.

**Healthcare Industry**

Healthcare professionals are entitled to rights

regarding the working time directive, which includes rules on maximum shift lengths and the minimum rest period between shifts. They are also entitled to rights pertinent to training and professional development.

**Education Sector**

Teachers have rights concerning maximum working hours and planning, preparation, and assessment (PPA) time. The School Teacher's Pay and Conditions Document (STPCD) also outlines their specific rights related to pay and conditions.

**Hospitality Industry**

Workers in the hospitality industry, including thsoe on zero-hour contracts, have rights to the National Minimum Wage, paid holiday, rest breaks, and protection against discrimination.

**Agriculture Industry**

Agricultural workers in England are granted specific rights related to pay, training, and accommodation as per the Agricultural Wages (England and Wales) Order.

**Transport & Logistics**

The EU Drivers' Hours rules and the Road Transport Working Time Regulations dictate specific rules related to working hours, rest breaks, and overnight accommodation for drivers.

**Retail**

Workers in the retail industry have the right to opt out of Sunday working at any time, subject to providing three months' notice.

# TEST YOURSELF

UK employment contracts, either written or verbal, are legally binding agreements that detail the terms of employment, rights, and responsibilities of both the employer and employee. These contracts typically include information about the job role, pay, working hours, holiday and sick leave entitlements, notice periods, and termination conditions. Employees' rights, such as a safe work environment, minimum wage, non-discrimination, and the right to join a trade union, among others, are also outlined. In addition, contracts may include industry-specific requirements. Both parties must adhere to these terms, with employers also obligated to respect employees' rights and ensure a safe work environment.

UK employment contracts often detail grievance procedures and disciplinary rules, including how an employee can raise a concern or complaint and the process the employer will follow. They also map out the consequences of breaching the contract terms, which could range from disciplinary action to termination. Confidentiality clauses and non-compete agreements may protect the employer's business interests and the employee's rights. Therefore, it is crucial for both parties to thoroughly understand and agree to the contract's contents before signing to ensure a fair and harmonious working relationship.

**COMPARE YOUR ANSWERS**

Example answers to these questions can be found in Appendix IV on Page 194

**1. What is an Employment Contract, and why is it significant in the UK?**

**2. What key elements must be included in an Employment Contract?**

3. **What rights do employees have under an Employment Contract in the UK?**

4. **Are there any industry-specific rights that employees should know?**

**5. Can the terms of an Employment Contract be changed after it has been signed?**

**6. What happens if an employer breaches the terms of an Employment Contract in the UK?**

**7. Does an Employment Contract need to be written and signed to be valid in the UK?**

**8. What steps should an employee take no written contract is received within two months of starting work?**

**9. Can an employee work for another employer under an Employment Contract?**

**10. How are Employment Contracts handled in the case of business mergers or takeovers in the UK?**

Ten Pounds
Bank of England

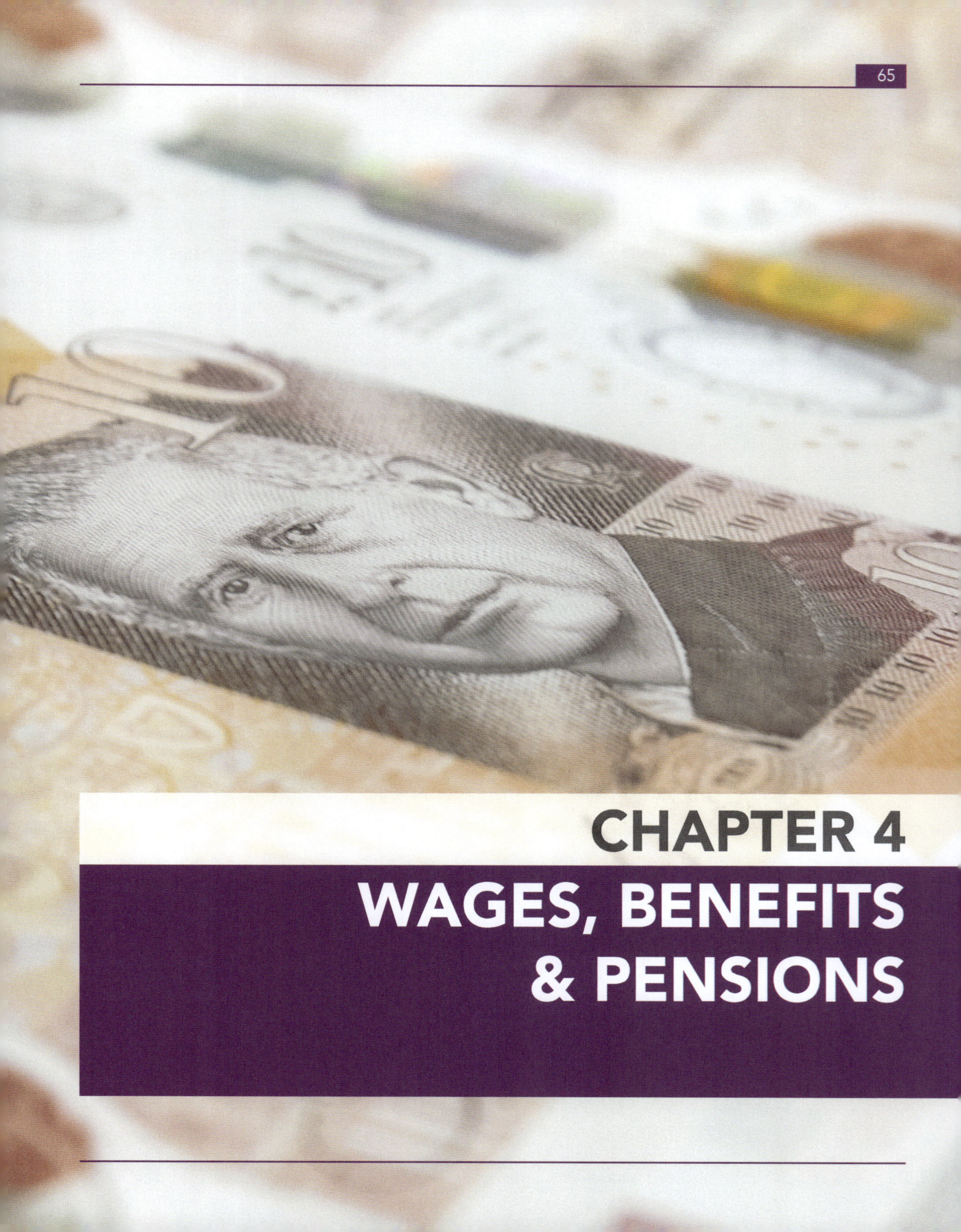

# CHAPTER 4
# WAGES, BENEFITS & PENSIONS

# MINIMUM WAGE LAWS

The UK is firmly committed to safeguarding employee rights, particularly around earnings. This dedication is evident in the country's robust laws concerning the minimum wage. These regulations guarantee that all workers, regardless of their industry or background, receive fair and adequate pay for their work.

The UK's minimum wage legislation primarily consists of the National Living Wage (NLW) and the National Minimum Wage (NMW). These rates are reviewed and updated annually, adjusted by economic factors. The rates vary based on the worker's age and whether they are an apprentice.

The NLW applies to workers aged 23 and over and is the higher of the two rates. The NMW, however, is broken down into different rates for various age groups and a separate rate for apprentices. The National Minimum Wage Act 1998 and the National Living Wage Regulations 2016 detail the UK's minimum wage laws. It is vital to understand how these rates are calculated and updated annually to ensure fair compensation for all eligible workers. These wage standards, set by the government, are crucial in establishing a foundation for employers when setting pay scales.

For instance, self-employed people, volunteers, company directors, and members of the armed forces are not entitled to the minimum wage. Additionally, some apprentices may earn less than the minimum wage depending on their age and how long they have been in their apprenticeship.

Non-compliance with the UK's minimum wage laws is a serious offence. Employers who fail to pay their workers minimum wage may face significant penalties, ranging from financial fines to criminal prosecution, depending on the violation's severity.

The UK's minimum wage laws play a vital role in safeguarding workers' rights and ensuring fair wages. Whether you are an employer or an employee or want to understand more about your rights and responsibilities, staying updated about these regulations is crucial. Understanding these laws can help avoid disputes and ensure all parties meet legal standards. Rates are updated annually, and the most cur rent rates can be found at https://www.gov.uk/national-minimum-wage-rates

**DID YOU KNOW?**
The enforcement of the UK's minimum wage laws is a crucial responsibility of HM Revenue and Customs (HMRC), an entity typically linked with tax collection. Employers who fail to meet minimum wage requirements can be subjected to immediate repayment of back wages and a potential fine of up to 200%, limited to £20,000 per worker. Such employers also face the prospect of public censure from the government. This enforcement intends to ensure that all workers receive the legally mandated fair pay.

Apart from the National Living Wage (NLW) and National Minimum Wage (NMW), the UK recognises the Real Living Wage, a voluntary rate by employers aiming for a living wage. Considering the cost of living, the Living Wage Foundation sets this rate and is adopted by over 7,000 UK businesses.

The Advisory, Conciliation and Arbitration Service (ACAS) offers employers and employees free and impartial information and advice on all workplace relations and employment law aspects. This includes guiding individuals on steps they can take if they believe they are underpaid. However, ACAS does not directly provide legal advice to underpaid workers. Instead, they can assist in resolving disputes between employers and employees.

**CURRENT NATIONAL MINIMUM WAGE**
As of April 2023

**£10.42 per hour**
Persons aged 23 or over

**£10.18 per hour**
Persons aged 21 or 22

**£7.49 per hour**
Persons aged 18 to 20

**£5.28 per hour**
Persons under 18 and apprentices under 19 or in first year of apprenticeship.

# NATIONAL MINIMUM WAGE HISTORY

The journey of the minimum wage in the UK began in 1999 when the government launched the National Minimum Wage (NMW) as a safeguard against unduly low wages. Changes to rates are guided by the independent Low Pay Commission.

**April 1999 - October 2004**

The initial rate was set at £3.60 for adults and £3.00 for those aged 18-21. This was the UK's first wage floor, ensuring a baseline level of compensation for workers.

**October 2004 - October 2010**

The introduction of a separate National Minimum Wage (NMW) for under-18s in October 2004 was an essential step in recognising the employment rights of young workers in the UK. It helped ensure younger employees received a fair wage for their work while also considering their relative inexperience and the potential impact of this on their employment opportunities.

**October 2010 - April 2016**

The introduction of a separate National Minimum Wage (NMW) for apprentices in October 2010 was a significant development in the UK's wage history.

It recognised the unique position of apprentices typically in a learning phase. This specific rate aimed to ensure fair pay for apprentices while encouraging more employers to provide apprenticeship opportunities.

**April 2016 - April 2021**

While the UK already had a National Minimum Wage (NMW) for all workers by 2016, there was criticism over insufficient living wages. To address this, a higher National Living Wage (NLW) was introduced for those aged 25 and over.

**April 2021 - Present**

In 2021, the UK expanded the National Living Wage (NLW) to include employees aged 23 and over, up from 25. Based on economic conditions, future plans may suggest lowering this age threshold to 21 by 2024.

**DID YOU KNOW?**

Before the UK's National Minimum Wage (NMW) of 1999, wage regulation primarily depended on collective bargaining between employers, trade unions, and individual agreements. The first wage regulation emerged in the 19th century, the "Truck Acts", requiring wages to be paid in legal currency, not goods or services.

Attempts to regulate wages during the Industrial Revolution through "Wages Councils" were largely unsuccessful, leading to their abolition by the late 1980s. The absence of a statutory minimum wage often resulted in low pay and exploitation, particularly in unskilled jobs, with women frequently earning less than men for the same work.

# TABLE OF NATIONAL MINIMUM WAGE RATES

<table>
<tr><th>Age:</th><th>25+</th><th>24</th><th>23</th><th>22</th><th>21</th><th>20</th><th>19</th><th>18</th><th>17</th><th>16</th><th>APP</th></tr>
<tr><td>1999 Apr</td><td colspan="4">£3.60</td><td colspan="4">£3.00</td><td colspan="3">n/a</td></tr>
<tr><td>2000 Oct</td><td colspan="4">£3.70</td><td colspan="4">£3.20</td><td colspan="3">n/a</td></tr>
<tr><td>2001 Oct</td><td colspan="4">£4.10</td><td colspan="4">£3.50</td><td colspan="3">n/a</td></tr>
<tr><td>2002 Oct</td><td colspan="4">£4.20</td><td colspan="4">£3.50</td><td colspan="3">n/a</td></tr>
<tr><td>2003 Oct</td><td colspan="4">£4.50</td><td colspan="4">£3.80</td><td colspan="3">n/a</td></tr>
<tr><td>2004 Oct</td><td colspan="4">£4.85</td><td colspan="4">£4.10</td><td colspan="2">£3.00</td><td>n/a</td></tr>
<tr><td>2005 Oct</td><td colspan="4">£5.05</td><td colspan="4">£4.25</td><td colspan="2">£3.00</td><td>n/a</td></tr>
<tr><td>2006 Oct</td><td colspan="4">£5.35</td><td colspan="4">£4.45</td><td colspan="2">£3.40</td><td>n/a</td></tr>
<tr><td>2007 Oct</td><td colspan="4">£5.52</td><td colspan="4">£4.60</td><td colspan="2">£3.53</td><td>n/a</td></tr>
<tr><td>2008 Oct</td><td colspan="4">£5.73</td><td colspan="4">£4.70</td><td colspan="2">£3.53</td><td>n/a</td></tr>
<tr><td>2009 Oct</td><td colspan="4">£5.80</td><td colspan="4">£4.83</td><td colspan="2">£3.57</td><td>n/a</td></tr>
<tr><td>2010 Oct</td><td colspan="5">£5.93</td><td colspan="3">£4.92</td><td colspan="2">£3.64</td><td>£2.50</td></tr>
<tr><td>2011 Oct</td><td colspan="5">£6.08</td><td colspan="3">£4.98</td><td colspan="2">£3.68</td><td>£2.60</td></tr>
<tr><td>2012 Oct</td><td colspan="5">£6.19</td><td colspan="3">£4.98</td><td colspan="2">£3.68</td><td>£2.65</td></tr>
<tr><td>2013 Oct</td><td colspan="5">£6.31</td><td colspan="3">£5.03</td><td colspan="2">£3.72</td><td>£2.68</td></tr>
<tr><td>2014 Oct</td><td colspan="5">£6.50</td><td colspan="3">£5.13</td><td colspan="2">£3.79</td><td>£2.73</td></tr>
<tr><td>2015 Oct</td><td colspan="5">£6.70</td><td colspan="3">£5.30</td><td colspan="2">£3.87</td><td>£3.30</td></tr>
<tr><td>2016 Apr</td><td>£7.20</td><td colspan="4">£6.70</td><td colspan="3">£5.30</td><td colspan="2">£3.87</td><td>£3.30</td></tr>
<tr><td>2016 Oct</td><td>£7.20</td><td colspan="4">£6.95</td><td colspan="3">£5.55</td><td colspan="2">£4.00</td><td>£3.40</td></tr>
<tr><td>2017 Apr</td><td>£7.50</td><td colspan="4">£7.05</td><td colspan="3">£5.60</td><td colspan="2">£4.05</td><td>£3.50</td></tr>
<tr><td>2018 Apr</td><td>£7.83</td><td colspan="4">£7.38</td><td colspan="3">£5.90</td><td colspan="2">£4.20</td><td>£3.70</td></tr>
<tr><td>2019 Apr</td><td>£8.21</td><td colspan="4">£7.70</td><td colspan="3">£6.15</td><td colspan="2">£4.35</td><td>£3.90</td></tr>
<tr><td>2020 Apr</td><td>£8.72</td><td colspan="4">£8.20</td><td colspan="3">£6.45</td><td colspan="2">£4.55</td><td>£4.15</td></tr>
<tr><td>2021 Apr</td><td colspan="3">£8.91</td><td colspan="2">£8.36</td><td colspan="3">£6.56</td><td colspan="2">£4.62</td><td>£4.30</td></tr>
<tr><td>2022 Apr</td><td colspan="3">£9.50</td><td colspan="2">£9.18</td><td colspan="3">£6.83</td><td colspan="2">£4.81</td><td>£4.81</td></tr>
<tr><td>2023 Apr</td><td colspan="3">£10.42</td><td colspan="2">£10.18</td><td colspan="3">£7.49</td><td colspan="2">£5.28</td><td>£5.28</td></tr>
</table>

# OVERTIME & HOLIDAY PAY

In the UK, the rules and regulations concerning overtime and holiday pay are guided by several key pieces of legislation, which protect workers' rights and ensure they receive appropriate compensation for their time.

**KEY LEGISLATION**

The principal laws include the Working Time Regulations 1998 and the Employment Rights Act 1996. The Health and Safety at Work, etc. Act 1974 is enacted to guarantee that employees are not exposed to health risks due to excessive working hours. The Working Time Regulations 1998 asserts that each worker is entitled to a minimum of 5.6 weeks of paid leave per year.

This type of leave can encompass public and bank holidays, as specified in the employment contract.

Calculating holiday pay can be complex. By law, holiday pay should reflect a worker's 'normal remuneration', which encompasses more than the basic salary. In other words, 'normal remuneration' includes all a worker's regular earnings.

This refers to the basic compensation received each pay period and considers a broader perspective of one's earnings. For instance, if you frequently work overtime and receive additional pay for those hours, this should be regarded as part of your 'normal remuneration'.

This also applies to any commission you earn on your standard salary. If you are in a sales role and regularly earn a commission, this should be included in your holiday pay calculation.

Moreover, other allowances that form part of your earnings, such as bonuses, meal allowances, or travel allowances, should also be factored into your holiday pay calculation if they are a regular component of your earnings. Considering the full range of your regular payments, not just your primary salary, is crucial when calculating holiday pay. This ensures that your holiday pay accurately reflects your usual earnings.

In the UK, employers are not legally required to pay extra for overtime work. It is often a voluntary choice by employers to offer higher pay rates for overtime. If an employer decides to provide this, the details, including the pay rate and definition of 'overtime', are usually specified in the employment contract, which is legally binding. Therefore, any mentioned conditions or benefits, including overtime pay, should be mutually respected.

Examining your employment contract closely would be beneficial to determine your potential eligibility for overtime pay. This crucial document will likely have all the required details about your wage, working hours, and any provisions for overtime pay. Understanding your contract will empower you to negotiate better terms and ensure you are adequately compensated for your work.

If you are still trying to decide after reviewing your agreement, or if the terms need clarification, it is always a good idea to consult an HR representative at your workplace or seek legal advice.

Knowing your overtime and holiday pay rights is crucial to ensuring fair treatment at work. By acquainting yourself with the laws that govern these areas, you can better navigate the issues that might arise. These rights are enshrined in UK law and can be referred to for clarity and resolution in case of any disputes. Moreover, being well-informed can strengthen your position if you ever need to negotiate or advocate for your rights.

**DID YOU KNOW?**

The concept of overtime pay in the UK dates back to the Industrial Revolution, with the Factory Act of 1850 setting the initial working hour restrictions. The idea of paid 'overtime' became widespread in the early 20th century. The Holidays with Pay Act 1938 recommended a week's holiday for workers, but the Working Time Regulations 1998 established a statutory right to at least 5.6 weeks of paid holiday. In a significant advancement in labour rights, the European Court of Justice's landmark Bear Scotland Ltd v. Fulton and Baxter; Hertel (UK) Ltd v. Wood and others; Amec Group Ltd v. Law and others ruling in 2014 mandated that holiday pay must include regular overtime hours.

# PENSIONS & BENEFITS

Navigating through the intricate world of pensions and employee benefits can seem daunting due to their complex nature and the extensive employment law framework in the UK. However, these complexities can be simplified with some explanation.

In the UK, it is a legal requirement for employers to establish a workplace pension scheme for their eligible employees. View a workplace pension as a retirement savings account. A certain percentage of an employee's earnings is automatically transferred into this account every pay period to ensure their financial stability after retirement. Workplace pensions are diverse—they are mainly categorised into two types: defined benefit schemes and defined contribution schemes.

A 'defined benefit' scheme promises a specific income once you retire, calculated based on factors like your earnings record and the duration of your contributions to the scheme. Conversely, a 'defined contribution' scheme does not assure a fixed amount. Instead, the amount you receive upon retirement depends on the total contributions made over your employment and the performance of the scheme's investments.

Employers carry specific responsibilities regarding these pension schemes. They must ensure that all eligible employees are enrolled in the system, make contributions to it, and must manage it effectively to protect the right and interests of their employees.

Let us delve into the People's Pension and the state pension and why they are essential. The People's Pension is a defined contribution scheme managed by a not-for-profit organisation. It provides employees with a straightforward, low-cost method to save for retirement. It is open to all workers, regardless of their income level or type of employment, hence the name People's Pension. On the other hand, the state pension is a regular payment made by the UK government to those who have reached the State Pension age. National Insurance contributions fund it and provide a basic income for people in retirement. This ensures a reliable source of income for those no longer working, reducing poverty and guaranteeing a decent quality of life in old age.

In the UK, fundamental worker rights are mandated by law, but employers often offer a range of additional employee benefits. These benefits can significantly vary depending on the job role. While the National Health Service (NHS) provides healthcare for all UK residents, some employers offer private health insurance as an extra benefit. This can give the employees quicker access to specialists, private hospitals, or treatments not covered by the NHS.

Many employers offer paid time off beyond the statutory annual leave. This could include additional holiday days, paid volunteer time, or personal days. Some companies provide pension schemes beyond the required state pension contributions.

These can be defined benefits plans or defined contribution plans. Other benefits include bonus schemes, company cars, subsidised meals, gym memberships, and childcare vouchers. The specifics and availability of these benefits can vary significantly from one role to another and from one company to another. Therefore, employees should always carefully review their employment contract or consult with their employer to understand the full range of benefits available in their role. Remember, pensions and benefits can sometimes be subject to changes in government policy, so it is always a good idea to stay informed about any updates or changes to the law.

**DID YOU KNOW?**

Under the Pensions Act 2008, every employer must auto-enrol specific staff into a pension scheme and contribute towards it. The eligibility criteria for automatic enrolment include being between the ages of 22 and State Pension age and earning at least £10,000 annually, provided that you usually or ordinarily work in the UK.

The pension scheme incorporates contributions from the employee, the employer, and tax relief from the government, thereby enhancing your retirement savings.

# TEST YOURSELF

UK Employment Law, essential for employers and employees, governs wages, benefits, and worker rights. It includes a variable National Minimum Wage and a Living Wage for those aged 23 and over. While it addresses overtime, extra pay is not always legally required. Full-time workers are entitled to at least 28 days of paid holiday, and employers must enrol eligible employees into a workplace pension scheme, making minimum contributions. The law also covers benefits like Statutory Sick Pay and maternity/paternity/adoption leave, with specifics often dependent on various factors.

In addition to these core provisions, UK employment law stipulates bonuses and performance-related pay, allowing employers to reward their employees monetarily based on company or individual performance. The decree outlines the processes for pay increases, which can be found in the length of service, performance, or changes in the minimum wage. The law also dictates that employers must provide a detailed pay statement to their employees with each payment.

There are multiple types of pension schemes tailored to meet the varying needs of employees, including defined benefit and defined contribution schemes.

**COMPARE YOUR ANSWERS**

Example answers to these questions can be found in Appendix IV on Page 196

1. **What is the current (2023) National Minimum Wage for individuals aged 23 and over in the UK?**

2. **How has the National Minimum Wage in the UK evolved over the years?**

**3.** **Under UK employment law, are employers always required to pay employees extra for overtime work?**

**4.** **How does holiday pay work in the UK?**

**5. What are the employer's responsibilities concerning workplace pensions in the UK?**

**6. Are apprentices eligible for the UK National Minimum Wage?**

**7. How often is the National Minimum Wage revised in the UK?**

**8. Are part-time workers in the UK entitled to the same benefits as full-time workers?**

**9. If employees work on a public holiday, are they entitled to extra pay under UK employment law?**

**10. What happens if an employer does not comply with the legal requirements for pensions in the UK?**

MIND

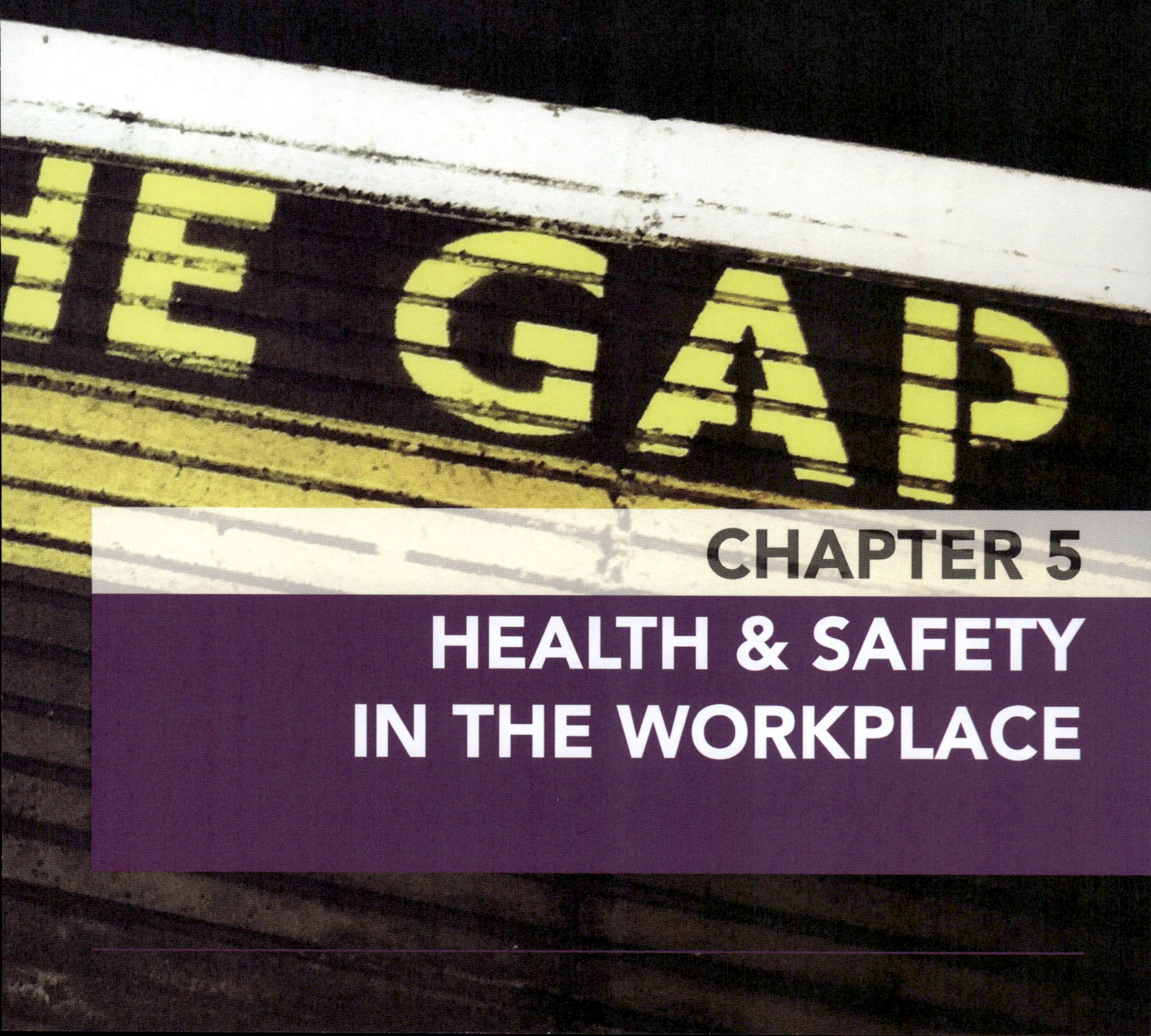

# CHAPTER 5

# HEALTH & SAFETY IN THE WORKPLACE

# EMPLOYEE RIGHTS & RESPONSIBILITIES

In the UK, a robust set of employment laws safeguard the rights and responsibilities of employees. These laws aim to create a safe and fair working environment for all. One of the fundamental rights of every employee is to work in an environment that does not jeopardise their health and safety. This is underpinned by the Health and Safety at Work Act 1974, which requires employers to ensure the well-being of their employees. This means, in practical terms, that employees have the legal right to refuse to perform work they perceive as unsafe. They can also report hazardous working conditions to their employer or the Health and Safety Executive (HSE), the UK's national workplace health and safety regulator.

Employees must responsibly balance their rights with their duties. This includes adhering to safety regulations, properly using safety equipment, and avoiding unnecessary risks. They should also support all employer-led health and safety measures, such as inspections, training, and use of protective gear. Misuse or interference with safety provisions, like fire extinguishers or alarms, can lead to legal repercussions. It is also worth noting that these rights and responsibilities apply regardless of an employee's employment category, whether full-time, part-time, temporary, or fixed-term. All employees are entitled to the same level of protection under UK employment law.

Under the umbrella of the Health and Safety at Work etc. Act 1974 has additional specific rights that cater to different work scenarios. For instance, employees who work with potentially harmful substances or in environments where they could be exposed to such chemicals have a right to be informed about these hazards. Employers are obliged to provide Safety Data Sheets detailing the properties of these substances, the health and safety precautions to be taken, and procedures to follow in an emergency. This ensures that employees can protect themselves appropriately when dealing with these substances.

Employees have the right to seek compensation following an accident resulting in injury or illness at work, provided the employer is proven to be at fault for violating their health and safety obligations. UK employers are mandated by the Employers' Liability (Compulsory Insurance) Act 1969 to have at least a minimum level of insurance, known as Employers' Liability Insurance. This insurance, which must provide a minimum cover of £5 million, ensures that funds are available to cover compensation claims.

**DID YOU KNOW?**
Under the Health and Safety at Work Act 1974 in the UK, employers must provide employees personal protective equipment (PPE) and clothing free of charge if there are health and safety risks that cannot be controlled or avoided by other means. This ensures the safety of employees while performing any potentially hazardous tasks.

# EMPLOYER OBLIGATIONS

In the UK, employers are legally obliged to adhere to stringent health and safety regulations to ensure a safe working environment. Their responsibilities are governed by the Health and Safety at Work etc. Act 1974 and subsequent rules are extensive and multifaceted.

First and foremost, employers must conduct comprehensive risk assessments to identify potential hazards within the workplace. This process involves thoroughly examining the work environment to determine situations or procedures that may cause harm, especially to those most at risk. It is not just about immediate physical risks; employers must also consider factors like work-related stress or exposure to harmful substances. Once these risks are identified, it is the employer's role to implement adequate safety measures to mitigate these risks. This could involve introducing new equipment, altering work processes, or even changing the physical layout of a workspace. Regular reviews and updates of these safety protocols are essential to ensure ongoing compliance and address emerging hazards.

In addition to ensuring physical safety measures, employers must equip their employees with the necessary knowledge and skills to work safely. This means providing comprehensive health and safety training, which should include correctly using any safety equipment and the procedures to follow in an emergency. Furthermore, UK law mandates employers to have employers liability insurance in place. This insurance provides cover in the event of an employee suffering injury or disease due to their work. Employers must also report specific types of workplace injuries, occupational illnesses and dangerous occurrences to the Health and Safety Executive (HSE), as per the Reporting of Injuries, Diseases and Dangerous Occurrences Regulations 2013 (RIDDOR).

It is important to note that these obligations apply to all employers, regardless of the size of the business or the employment category of the worker. Whether employees are full-time, part-time, temporary, or even self-employed but working on the business premises, employers still hold a duty of care to ensure their health and safety.

Beyond their legal duties, employers are urged to instil a proactive culture around health and safety within their organisation. This involves encouraging employees to voice concerns or suggestions about workplace safety, thereby ensuring a more effective identification and mitigation of health and safety risks. Employers could achieve this by setting up health and safety committees or appointing safety representatives, facilitating effective communication about these issues. Furthermore, employers are urged to pay attention to their workforce's mental health and well-being. This could involve supporting work-related stress, implementing flexible working hours, or providing access to counselling services. By taking such an all-encompassing approach towards health and safety, employers can ensure compliance with the law and enhance overall employee well-being, increasing productivity.

# WORKPLACE ACCIDENTS & ILLNESS

Managing workplace accidents and illnesses is an essential aspect of UK employment law. It provides a structured protocol that employers must follow when these unfortunate events occur.

Firstly, the employer must make immediate arrangements to ensure that the affected employee receives first aid. This step places the health of the employee as the utmost priority. The Health and Safety (First-Aid) Regulations 1981 mandates employers to provide adequate equipment and facilities to give first-aid to employees if they are injured or become ill at work.

In cases where the injury or illness is severe, employers are legally required to report the incident to the Health and Safety Executive (HSE), the UK body responsible for enforcing workplace health and safety regulations. The Reporting of Injuries, Diseases and Dangerous Occurrences Regulations 2013 (RIDDOR) sets this requirement, which includes reporting severe specific workplace accidents, occupational diseases, and near-miss incidents.

Every incident must be recorded in an 'accident book' for businesses with more than ten employees. This record demonstrates the company's commitment to safety and can be crucial if legal issues arise from the incident. Employers are also expected to comprehensively investigate incidents to identify potential risks or oversights that may have contributed to the accident or illness. This step is vital in preventing similar occurrences in the future.

Should an employee feel that their employer has not sufficiently addressed or resolved a safety concern, they are fully entitled to lodge a formal complaint with the Health and Safety Executive (HSE). This step can be crucial in preventing further breaches of health and safety regulations. It is essential to be aware that the Employers' Liability (Compulsory Insurance) Act 1969 stipulates employers must hold valid insurance to provide financial compensation for employees who become injured or ill due to their work.

In addition, employers must make their insurance certificate readily accessible to all employees by displaying it in a prominent location. Similarly, employers must also show the HSE-approved health and safety poster in a place readily visible to all employees, further ensuring awareness and adherence to health and safety guidelines.

**DID YOU KNOW?**

In 2021/22, 565,000 workers experienced non-fatal injuries at their workplaces. In a more heartbreaking statistic, workplace accidents claimed the lives of 123 workers within the same 12-month period. According to estimates, these non-fatal injuries resulted in approximately six million lost working days.

These numbers underscore the critical need for adequate safety measures and a focus on well-being withinthe workplace.

After an incident at the workplace, it is the employer's responsibility to modify either the workspace or the employee's role, provided the affected person can return to work. This could mean changing their working hours and duties or modifying the workspace to cater to their needs. As per the Equality Act 2010, employers must make reasonable adjustments to ensure employees are not disadvantaged if they are, or have become, disabled. To determine the most appropriate adjustments, employers are expected to hold discussions with the concerned employee and, if needed, their General Practitioner.

In addition to immediate response and reporting obligations, employers must implement ongoing health and safety measures to protect employees and prevent future incidents. This includes conducting regular risk assessments, providing necessary employee training, and implementing suitable health and safety policies. The Management of Health and Safety at Work act requires employers to assess risks to the health and safety of employees and make arrangements for implementing health and safety measures identified as necessary by the risk assessment.

Lastly, it is essential to note that while the employer is primarily responsible for ensuring workplace health and safety, employees also play a crucial role. They have to take care of their health and safety and others who may be affected by their actions at work. This includes cooperating with employers and co-workers to help everyone meet their legal requirements

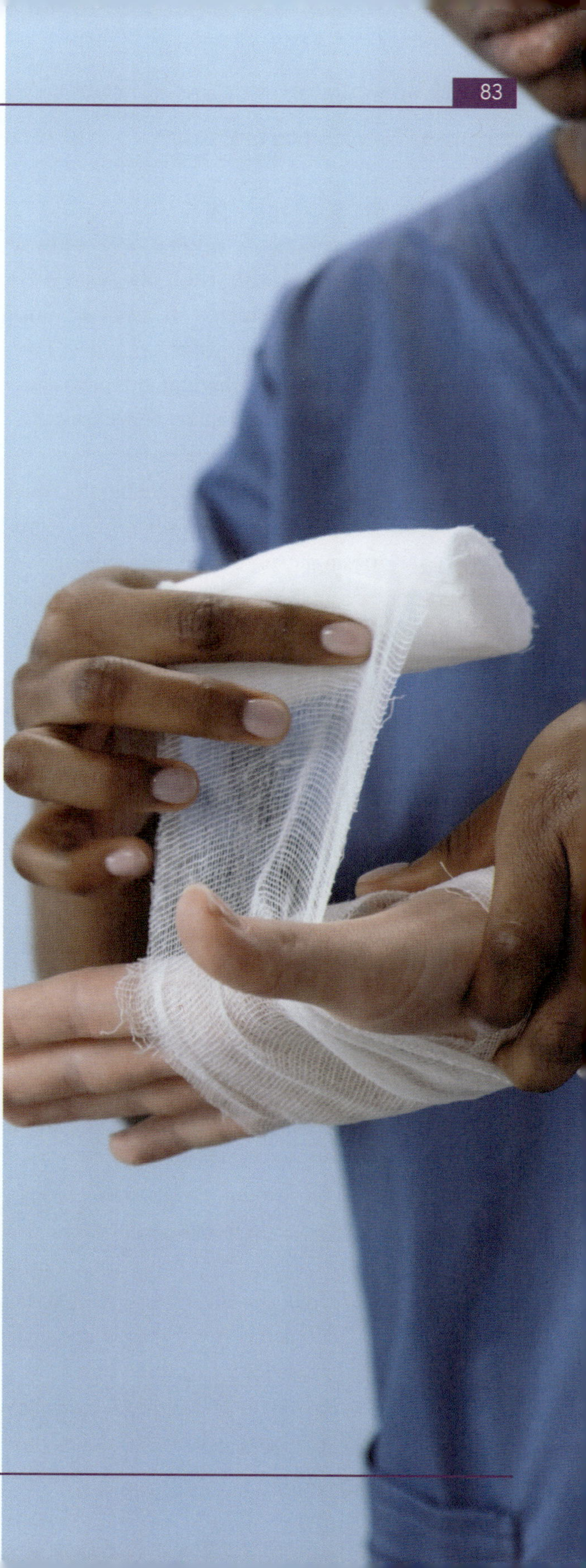

# TEST YOURSELF

In the UK, health and safety in the workplace is a significant aspect of employment law, with employers and employees having distinct rights and responsibilities. Employers must ensure a safe and healthy workplace per the Health and Safety at Work Act 1974, which includes providing necessary training, maintaining equipment, and implementing appropriate safety measures. They must also carry out regular risk assessments and have a written health and safety policy for businesses with five or more employees.

On the other hand, employees are responsible for following safety procedures and using provided safety equipment. In the event of workplace accidents or illnesses, employers may be liable if it is proven that they failed to uphold their health and safety obligations. Employers must also report specific workplace accidents, injuries, and illnesses to the Health and Safety Executive (HSE) under the Reporting of Injuries, Diseases and Dangerous Occurrences Regulations 2013 (RIDDOR).

Additionally, a company's adherence to the Health and Safety at Work Act 1974 and RIDDOR 2013 is subject to inspections by the HSE, which has the authority to enforce penalties for non-compliance, including fines and imprisonment.

**COMPARE YOUR ANSWERS**

Example answers to these questions can be found in Appendix IV on Page 198

1. **What are the primary responsibilities of an employer regarding health and safety in the workplace?**

2. **What rights do employees have concerning health and safety in the workplace?**

3. **What is an employer's duty in case of a workplace accident?**

4. **How can employers effectively reduce the risk of workplace illnesses?**

**5. What steps should employers take to fulfil their health and safety obligations?**

**6. Can employees refuse to work if they believe their workplace is unsafe?**

**7. Apart from providing a safe and healthy workplace, what other obligations does an employer have regarding health and safety?**

**8. What should an employer do if a worker becomes ill because of their work?**

**9. Is it an employer's responsibility to provide employees personal protective equipment (PPE)?**

**10. What are the potential consequences for an employer if they fail to comply with health and safety regulations?**

# CHAPTER 6
# RESOLVING ISSUES IN THE WORKPLACE

# COMMON EMPLOYMENT LAW ISSUES

The realm of UK employment law is an expansive and multifaceted one, where problems may inevitably surface within the professional environment. Some of the most frequently encountered issues revolve around unfair dismissals, discrimination, wage disputes, and matters related to employment contracts.

Unfair dismissals occur when an employee's contract is terminated without a legitimate, justifiable reason or adherence to the correct procedural steps. As outlined in the Employment Rights Act 1996, an employer must have a fair reason (like redundancy, misconduct, or incapability) for dismissing an employee. Also, they must act reasonably during the dismissal process.

Conversely, discrimination is the unjust or prejudiced treatment of employees based on protected characteristics such as race, age, gender, religion, or disability, as stated in the Equality Act 2010. This law ensures that every employee has the right to be treated fairly in the workplace, and employers who fail to adhere to these guidelines can face severe penalties.

Wage disputes often emerge from disagreements between employers and employees over the remuneration for work done. This could include disputes over the minimum wage, regulated in the UK by the National Minimum Wage Act 1998, or disagreements over overtime pay. Issues related to employment contracts often stem from misunderstandings or breaches of contractual terms. These contracts, which should clearly outline the terms and conditions of an individual's employment, are regulated under the Employment Rights Act 1996.

It is also worth noting the distinction between different categories of employment in the UK - employees, workers, and self-employed - as each category comes with other rights and protections. For instance, 'employees' have all the rights workers do but can also claim unfair dismissal, statutory redundancy pay and minimum notice periods, which 'workers' cannot. Understanding these common employment law issues, the relevant laws, and employment categories can empower employers and workers, leading to more harmonious workplace relations.

One area where disputes frequently arise is with working hours and rest breaks. According to the Working Time Regulations 1998, workers have the right to limit the maximum number of hours they can work in a week and entitlement to rest

**DID YOU KNOW?**
Under the Working Time Regulations 1998, employees working more than six hours daily are entitled to a minimum 20-minute uninterrupted rest break in the UK.

However, some workers, including self-employed individuals, certain emergency services and domestic servants, may fall under exceptions to the regulations.

breaks and paid leave. However, there can often be confusion or disagreements over how these rules should be applied, especially in sectors where flexible or atypical working patterns are the norm.

Another common issue pertains to whistleblowing. The law protects workers who disclose workplace malpractice information, provided the disclosure meets specific criteria under the Public Interest Disclosure Act 1998. There can often be disputes about whether a worker has made a protected disclosure and whether any subsequent action by the employer constitutes unlawful detriment or dismissal.

Bullying and harassment is another prevalent issue in the workplace. The Equality Act 2010 prohibits harassment related to any of the protected characteristics. However, it can sometimes be challenging to establish what constitutes bullying or harassment, and employees may feel uncertain about their rights and how to address such behaviour.

Lastly, redundancy and business reorganisation are other areas where disputes are common. The Employer Rights Act 1996 stipulates that redundancies must be carried out fairly - this includes proper consultation, using fair criteria for redundancy selection, and considering suitable alternative employment. Misunderstandings or breaches of these obligations by employers can lead to disputes and potential employment tribunal claims.

# COMMUNICATION & NEGOTIATION

Effective communication and negotiation are critical in addressing and resolving employment law issues in the UK. A business, regardless of its size, should strive to foster a culture where open and sincere communication is not just encouraged but is a fundamental principle.

This involves openly sharing the company's policies, conduct standards, and employee expectations. Employers need to promptly communicate any changes that may impact employees, such as updates to company policies or alternations in working conditions. This aligns with the Employment Rights Act 1996, which mandates employers to provide employees with a written statement of employment terms within two months of their start date. This statement should detail employment conditions, including wage rates, working hours, holiday entitlement, and notice periods for termination.

Negotiation is central when dealing with issues like wage disputes or contract modifications. For instance, while the National Minimum Wage Act 1998 sets legally enforceable minimum wage rates, there may be situations where employees believe they merit more due to the nature of their job or their level of experience.

In such cases, negotiation can provide a platform for employees to voice their viewpoints and employers to reconsider their wage policies to satisfy both parties. Understanding that employment classification can significantly impact the negotiation process is essential. In the UK, 'workers', which include employees and certain contractors, have fewer statutory rights than 'employees'. These rights include the right to a minimum notice period if their employment ends, the right to maternity, paternity or adoption leave, and the right to request flexible working. Recognising these distinctions can help guide the negotiation towards a fair and lawful resolution.

While cultivating a culture of effective communication and skilled negotiation is beneficial, it is not a comprehensive substitute for legal advice or action when necessary. Complex disputes or serious allegations, such as discrimination or unfair dismissal, may necessitate the intervention of an employment tribunal or a legal professional.

Moreover, it is equally essential for employees to actively voice their concerns, understand their rights, and seek advice if they feel their rights have been violated. In essence, while direct communication and negotiation should be the first steps in resolving employment law issues, legal proceedings may still be necessary in some cases. However, prioritising communication and negotiation can help reduce the need for such proceedings, thus saving time and expense and preserving positive employer-employee relationships.

Building upon the principles of communication and negotiation, establishing robust feedback mechanisms can further enhance the work environment. These mechanisms should provide employees with a safe and confidential platform to voice their concerns or issues without fear of retaliation. They could be suggestion boxes, regular surveys, or one-on-one meetings with management. This openness not only keeps employers informed about potential issues but also reinforces the culture of open communication. It demonstrates to employees that their voices are heard and their opinions valued, which can significantly impact employee morale, productivity, and job satisfaction.

In addition to in-house efforts, it may benefit businesses to incorporate external resources to support their workforce further. This could include partnerships with legal advisory services or counselling programs to provide additional support to employees. Legal advice can help employees better understand their rights and entitlements while counselling services can help them manage workplace stress or conflict. Such initiatives demonstrate the employer's commitment to ensuring a fair and supportive work environment. They also help mitigate potential legal issues by equipping employees with the necessary knowledge and tools to address their concerns.

Furthermore, regular training and development programs can create a more harmonious workplace. These programs could cover topics such as understanding employment law, effective communication, conflict resolution, and negotiation techniques. Businesses can foster a more collaborative culture by equipping both employers and employees with these skills. This not only aids in the swift resolution of any potential issues but also helps to prevent disputes from arising in the first place. Ultimately, these proactive steps can improve workplace relations and reduce the need for more drastic legal interventions.

**DID YOU KNOW?**

Reflective Listening is a communication technique used globally, including in the UK. It involves understanding a speaker's idea and replaying it back for clarity.

While its effectiveness in UK employment can vary, it is a valuable tool for skilfully enhancing communication and negotiation.

# MEDIATION, CONCILIATION & ARBITRATION

When communication breaks down or negotiations stall in UK employment disputes, two frequently used alternative dispute resolution methods are mediation and conciliation.

Mediation involves a neutral third party, the mediator, who facilitates the conversation between the disputing parties. The mediator's role is not to impose decisions but rather to guide discussions to help parties understand each other's viewpoints and potentially reach a mutually acceptable resolution. The parties aim to create solutions catering to their individual needs.

Conciliation is a similar process but involves the third party, the conciliator, taking a more active role. Beyond facilitating discussions, the conciliator proposes potential resolution suggestions and may even nudge the parties towards a compromise. The conciliator takes an active role in helping to establish an agreement that satisfies both parties.

Mediation and conciliation are confidential procedures providing a secure open discussion space. These processes are less formal and usually quicker than court proceedings, offering a cost-effective alternative. However, while mediation and conciliation are confidential, any agreements reached and formalised in writing can become legally binding if signed by all parties.

A distinct aspect of UK employment law categorises employees and workers, each possessing different rights and protections. This distinction can impact the management of disputes and the appropriateness of resolution methods. Mediation and conciliation are crucial tools in UK employment law. Being less adversarial, they assist in preserving the working relationship between parties and can alleviate the stress often associated with legal disputes. However, these methods may only sometimes be suitable or effective depending on the nature of the dispute, the relationship between the parties, and their willingness to participate in these processes. Professional legal advice should always be sought to ensure adherence to UK laws and protect the rights of all parties involved. If the dispute cannot be resolved via these methods, the case may need to go to an Employment Tribunal or court.

Complementing mediation and conciliation, arbitration is another alternative dispute resolution method prevalent in the UK employment law spectrum. Similar to mediation and conciliation, arbitration involves a neutral third party. However, the arbitrator can decide legally on the dispute after hearing evidence from both sides. This method is often used when parties desire a definitive resolution but wish to avoid court proceedings' formalities, public nature, and potential costs. It is crucial, though, that both parties agree to the arbitration process as the decision is final and, hence, has limited scope for appeal.

A significant aspect of these alternative dispute resolution methods lies in their flexibility. Unlike rigid court procedures, these methods allow for tailored approaches to individual cases. The neutral third party, whether a mediator, conciliator, or arbitrator, can adapt the process to suit the nature of the dispute, the relationship between the parties, and their respective needs and interests. This flexibility can enhance communication and understanding, facilitating more satisfying and sustainable resolutions. Despite the benefits of these methods, it is important to note that they may only be suitable for some employment disputes. For instance, severe misconduct or complex legal issues may require a more formal process and judgment. In such circumstances, Employment Tribunals or courts may be more appropriate for ensuring justice and upholding the parties' rights.

UK trade unions play a critical role in worker representation during employment disputes, offering supportive advice and influencing the dispute resolution method. Their involvement brings an additional layer of complexity to the dispute resolution process.

**DID YOU KNOW?**
The Advisory, Conciliation and Arbitration Service (ACAS), an autonomous public entity, is a part of the UK's employment law framework. This organisation delivers unbiased and complimentary counsel to employers, workers, and their delegates regarding employment rights, optimal methods, and regulations. It extends a distinctive service termed 'Early Conciliation'.

# TEST YOURSELF

Resolving issues in the workplace involves identifying conflicts or disagreements, whether between employees or between management and staff and then taking steps to deal with these issues effectively. Proper resolution can prevent escalating conflicts, reduce stress and tension, and ensure a more harmonious working environment. Common employment law issues may include unfair dismissal, discrimination, contract breach, or pay and benefits issues. These issues are regulated by employment law to protect the rights of employees and employers. Communication and negotiation are crucial to managing workplace disputes.

Clear and open communication can help understand the position of all parties involved, and negotiation can help reach a mutually acceptable resolution. Mediation and conciliation are forms of alternative dispute resolution that are often used to resolve workplace disputes. Mediation involves a neutral third party who helps the disputing parties to reach an agreement. At the same time, conciliation is a more formal process where the conciliator may propose a resolution. Both methods are designed to resolve disputes less confrontational and more constructively.

**COMPARE YOUR ANSWERS**
Example answers to these questions can be found in Appendix IV on Page 200

1. **According to UK employment law, what is the first step to take if an issue arises in the workplace?**

2. **What is one of the UK's most common employment law issues?**

**3.** **How important is communication and negotiation in resolving workplace disputes?**

**4.** **What is the role of mediation in employment issues?**

**5. How does conciliation differ from mediation in employment law?**

**6. What are some key elements that should be considered when resolving issues in the workplace?**

**7. What methods prevent common employment law issues?**

**8. How can negotiation skills be improved for better communication in the workplace?**

9. **What is the mediation process for employment disputes?**

10. **Can an employee refuse to participate in conciliation?**

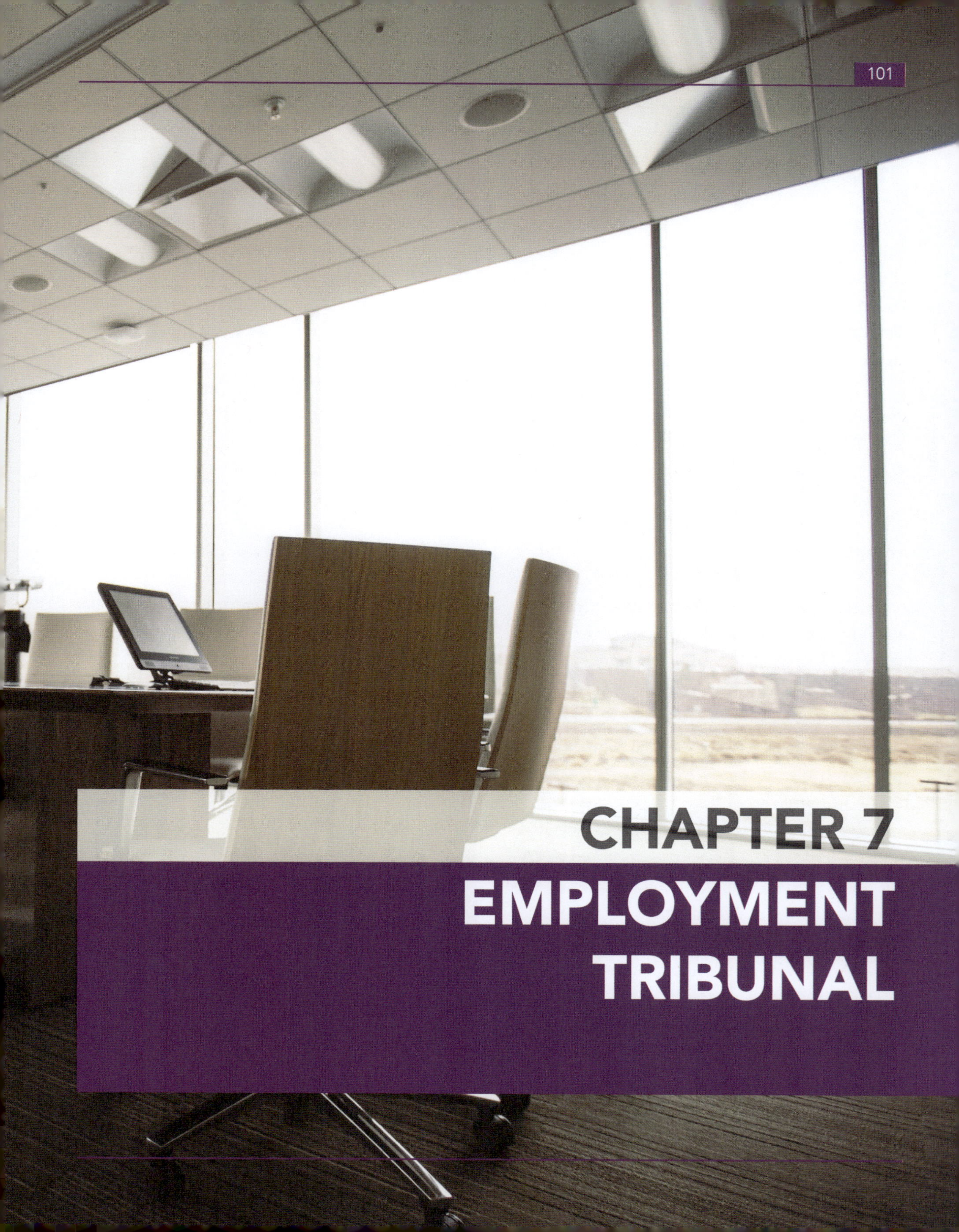

# CHAPTER 7
# EMPLOYMENT TRIBUNAL

# WHEN & WHY TO GO

An Employment Tribunal is an independent judicial body in the UK designed to resolve disputes between employers and employees concerning employment rights. It is a court of law, albeit less formal than others, and its rulings are legally binding. Before considering the Employment Tribunal, it is essential to understand that it is typically viewed as a final measure to be used when all other resolution methods have been exhausted. Such methods can include internal grievance procedures, where the issue is raised and handled within the organisation, or mediation, where a neutral third party helps to negotiate a resolution.

An employee may may need to resort to an Employment Tribunal if they have experienced unfair dismissal, discrimination, or non-payment of due wages or benefits. Unfair dismissal could be a scenario where an employee has been let go without a valid reason or following the correct procedure. Discrimination covers issues related to gender, race, disability, age, religion, or sexual orientation under the Equality Act 2010. Non-payment of wages or benefits could involve not receiving the national minimum wage, holiday pay, or legally due overtime.

In the UK, employment status is categorised into 'employees', 'workers', and 'self-employed', each having different employment rights. Employees have full employment rights, workers have some rights (like the national minimum wage and statutory minimum holiday), while self-employed people have few employment rights. So, applying your rights and the relevancy of the Employment Tribunal can depend on your employment status.

Any infringement of your employment rights under UK law can be grounds for a tribunal. Understanding when and why to go to an Employment Tribunal is crucial; it helps safeguard your rights and maintains a healthy work environment.

The Employment Tribunal operates in a two-tier system. The 'First-tier Tribunal' hears most cases initially, and decisions from this level can be appealed to the 'Upper Tribunal'. The First-tier Tribunal is divided into sections, each specialising in various disputes, such as unfair dismissal or discrimination. This ensures that a panel with the appropriate expertise hears each case. The Upper Tribunal mainly deals with appeals, where

**DID YOU KNOW?**
Established as Industrial Tribunals in 1964 and later renamed Employment Tribunals in 1998, these UK entities resolve employment disputes. They allow self-representation, which can benefit simple cases but may be challenging for complex ones or those unfamiliar with employment law.

Despite their informality compared to courts, their decisions are legally binding. For complex cases, professional legal advice is recommended.

it is claimed that the First-tier Tribunal made an error in law. It is crucial to note that pursuing a case through the Employment Tribunal can be time-consuming and stressful. From the moment you submit your claim, it can take several months, sometimes even a year or more, for your case to be heard. During this period, you may need to gather evidence, liaise with your employer, and negotiate an out-of-court settlement. It would be best to consider whether the potential outcome will justify the time and emotional investment required.

The Employment Tribunal aims to provide a fair, accessible way to resolve employment disputes, but it is not the only option. Alternatives include seeking resolution through trade unions, where applicable, or ACAS (Advisory, Conciliation and Arbitration Service). ACAS offers free advice and provides a mandatory Early Conciliation service that must be used before most types of cases can proceed to an Employment Tribunal. This service aims to resolve disputes without needing a formal court hearing.

While there are no fees to lodge a claim or response with the Employment Tribunal in the UK, there may be other costs. These could include travel expenses to attend hearings, loss of earnings due to time off work, and legal advice or representation expenses. Some individuals may be eligible for financial assistance through legal aid or their trade union. Considering these potential costs is crucial when deciding whether to proceed with an Employment Tribunal claim.

# THE TRIBUNAL PROCESS

The journey through an Employment Tribunal process in the UK can be complex and lengthy. However, a clear understanding of the procedure can help demystify the process and make it more manageable for employees and employers.

Each case before an Employment Tribunal is distinct and may not necessarily follow a set sequence of events. Resolution might be achieved through mediation, or a settlement could be reached before a case escalates to a full hearing. In some instances, additional steps may be involved, such as lodging appeals or initiating the ACAS early conciliation process. The latter is a compulsory preliminary stage for most Employment Tribunal claims.

Hence, it is always advisable for parties involved in an Employment Tribunal case, whether as an employer or an employee, to seek professional legal counsel. Grasping the legal complexities and procedural aspects of an Employment Tribunal can appear daunting, but with the right guidance and information, both employers and employees can effectively manage this process.

It is crucial to note that claims must typically be lodged **within three months**, minus one day of the incident.

**1. Initiation of the Claim by Employee**

The legal process begins when the employee initiates a claim by completing a form known as an **E11**. In this form, the employee outlines the specifics of their dispute with the employer, which could encompass issues like wrongful dismissal, discrimination, or unfair treatment. Understanding the distinction between 'employees' and 'workers' under UK law is crucial, as the former category has more rights and protections, including the right to claim unfair dismissal.

**2. Employer Response**

Once the claim is received, the Employment Tribunal reviews it. If the claim is accepted, the employer is notified and given 28 days to respond. The employer submits their response using a form known as **ET3**, where they can either dispute the claim, accept liability, or argue that the tribunal lacks jurisdiction to hear the case.

**5. Judgment**

The judgment phase takes place after the hearing. The tribunal panel delivers its judgement, which could be announced verbally immediately after the hearing or may be reserved and provided later in written form to both parties involved. This judgment includes the final decision and the comprehensive reasoning that led to it. However, the specifics of the procedures can vary based on the unique circumstances of each case.

**4. Full Hearing**

The full hearing is the main event of the Tribunal process, during which both parties present their cases. This includes providing evidence, cross-examining witnesses, and making legal arguments. A panel, typically consisting of a legally qualified Employment Judge and possibly two lay members, considers the evidence presented.

**3. Preliminary Hearing**

If the case includes any ambiguities or complex issues, a preliminary hearing may be scheduled to clarify these matters, determine the direction of the case, and establish a timetable for the proceedings.

# OUTCOMES & IMPLICATIONS

Employment Tribunals, a significant judicial institution in the UK, are mandated to settle disputes between employers and employees. They play a crucial role in interpreting and applying UK employment law, which recognises various workers.

When the tribunal rules in favour of the employee, the impact on the employer can be significant—the employee might be awarded financial compensation, which is determined by factors such as the nature of the employer's transgression and the length of the employee's tenure. In instances of unjust dismissal, the tribunal might order the employee to be reinstated. However, this is rare and generally only occurs when the tribunal finds the dismissal extraordinarily unfair and the working relationship salvageable. Furthermore, the employer could be directed to revise their policies to align with employment law requirements. They might need to implement enhanced procedures for handling grievances or disciplinary issues or foster equal opportunities and prevent discrimination in the workplace. These updates are essential for legal compliance and fostering a more respectful and harmonious working environment. Conversely, if the tribunal rules in the employer's favour, the employee's claim has been dismissed. Although this could theoretically influence their current or future employment opportunities, it is not usually a significant concern.

Employment Tribunal decisions are public record but do not typically appear in standard background checks by employers unless the case has garnered considerable media attention.

Regarding employment categories, full-time employees might face a more significant impact than part-time or temporary workers due to their typically longer tenure and deeper involvement in their roles. In both scenarios, the parties could also incur costs related to the tribunal process. These could include legal fees and the potential loss of earnings due to time taken off work. The potential damage to the parties' reputations must be considered, especially for employers facing public scrutiny or a decrease in employee morale.

The impact of Employment Tribunals is not limited to the direct parties involved in the dispute. These decisions can have broader implications for industry standards and legal precedents. For instance, a tribunal ruling that interprets a particular aspect of employment law novelty could set a precedent that other employers in the sector must adhere to. This ripple effect underscores the importance of these tribunals in shaping the working landscape and the conditions of employment within the UK. The tribunal's decisions, particularly those that attract media attention, can inform public opinion on workers' rights and business ethics and influence the regulatory environment.

Employment Tribunals also play a significant role in promoting transparency and fairness within the UK's employment sector. They serve as a platform for employees to voice their grievances and hold employers accountable for their actions. This is especially important when power imbalances or fear of retaliation might otherwise prevent employees from raising concerns about their working conditions or treatment. By providing a formal, legal channel for these issues to be aired and addressed, tribunals contribute to the promotion of just and equitable workplaces.

In addition to interpreting and applying existing laws, tribunal rulings highlight areas where legislation may need to evolve to protect workers' rights better. For example, as the nature of work changes with advancements in technology and shifts in societal norms, new types of disputes between employers and employees may arise. The tribunals' handling of these cases can shed light on gaps in the current legal framework and prompt lawmakers to consider updates or additions to employment law.

Lastly, while the dispute resolution process can be stressful and time-consuming for both parties, Employment Tribunals are integral to maintaining trust between employers and employees. The awareness that a system is in place to handle and adjudicate disputes can give both parties confidence in their rights being upheld. This trust is crucial for fostering productive and respectful working relationships, contributing to the overall health and success of businesses and the satisfaction and well-being of their employees.

**DID YOU KNOW?**

UK Employment Tribunals are not just confined to the traditional brick-and-mortar courtroom. To accommodate the modern digital era and the challenges posed by the global pandemic, many tribunal hearings have taken place remotely via video conferencing platforms. This technological advancement allows for a more flexible and accessible approach to justice, ensuring that disputes can be heard and resolved promptly, irrespective of physical constraints.

# TEST YOURSELF

Employment tribunals in the UK are legal bodies designed to settle disputes between employers and employees regarding unfair dismissal, discrimination, and redundancy pay. Individuals may go to an employment tribunal when they believe their employment rights have been violated and they have not been able to resolve the issue through other means, such as mediation or internal procedures.

The tribunal process involves several stages, including making a claim, preparing for the hearing, and attending the hearing, which can be quite complex and typically requires legal advice. The outcomes of employment tribunals can have significant implications; if the tribunal rules in favour of the employee, they may be entitled to compensation or reinstatement in their job. At the same time, employers may face financial penalties and damage to their reputations.

It is critical to note that going to an employment tribunal can be lengthy, often taking several months or even years to conclude. Notwithstanding, employment tribunals play a crucial role in enforcing employment law and ensuring workplace justice, making them an essential aspect of the UK's labour structure.

**COMPARE YOUR ANSWERS**
Example answers to these questions can be found in Appendix IV on Page 202

1. **What is an employment tribunal, and when might someone need to use one?**

2. **How does the employment tribunal process work?**

**3.** **What can be the possible outcomes of an employment tribunal?**

**4.** **What are the implications of an employment tribunal for an employer?**

**5. When and why should an employee consider attending an employment tribunal?**

**6. Can anyone represent you at an employment tribunal?**

**7. How long does an employment tribunal process usually take?**

**8. What types of evidence are used in an employment tribunal process?**

9. **What happens if an employer does not comply with the outcome of an employment tribunal?**

10. **Can the decision of an employment tribunal be appealed?**

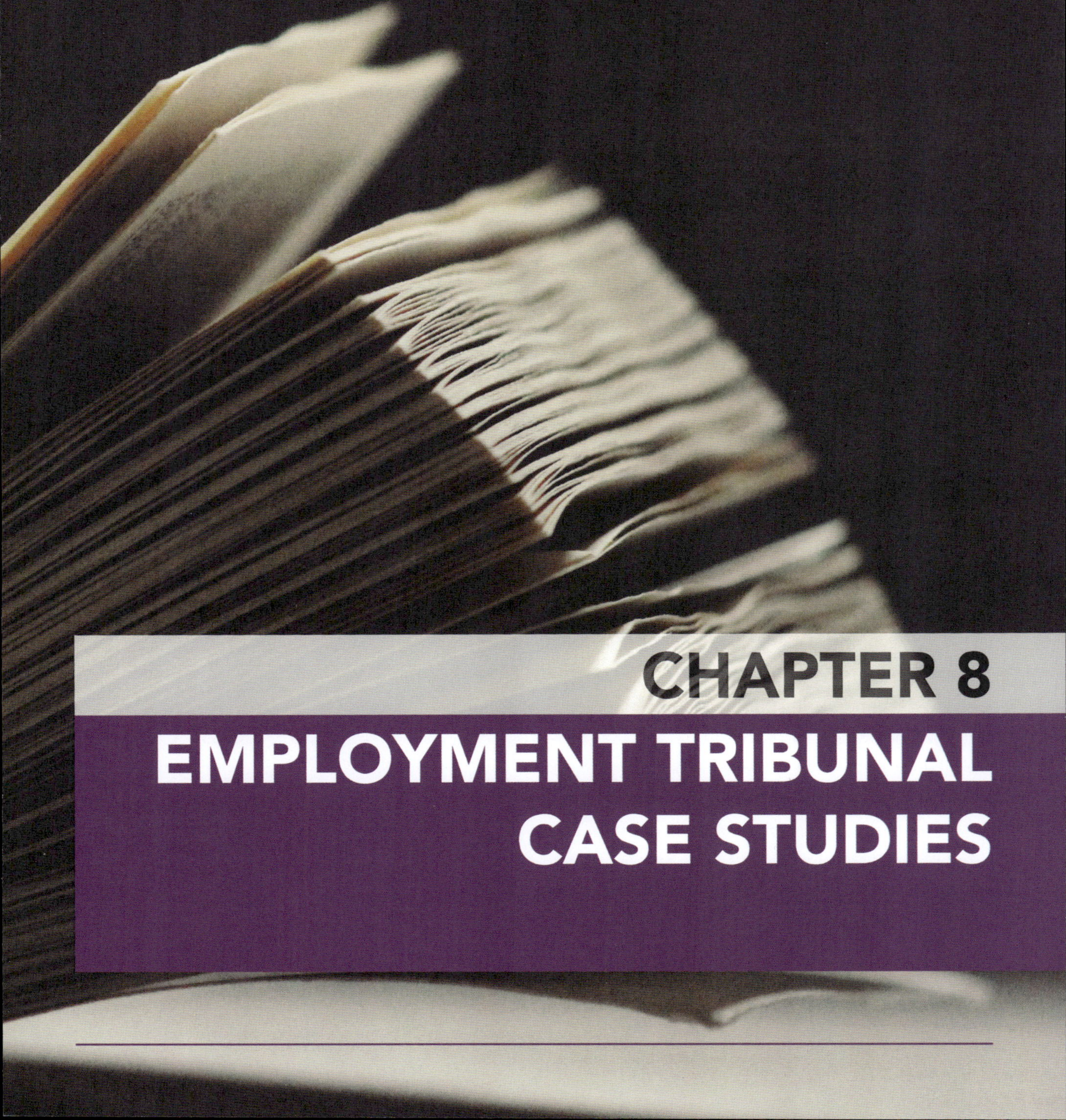

# CHAPTER 8

# EMPLOYMENT TRIBUNAL CASE STUDIES

# WILSON & OTHERS v. UNITED KINGDOM (2002)

This case involved disputes over pay negotiations, where the employees in question were sanctioned by their employers due to their involvement with trade unions. The European Court of Human Rights (ECHR) found the UK to violate Article 11 of the European Convention on Human Rights, which guarantees the right to freedom of assembly and association. The court held that the UK had failed to protect the employees and their trade unions from detrimental treatment by their employers.

Following the European Court of Human Rights ruling, the UK was faced with the urgent task of reviewing its legislation and mechanisms to protect workers' rights. The ECHR emphasised the importance of Article 11, which encompasses the right to join and participate in trade union activities without fear of retaliation or sanction. This case served as a reminder of the crucial role of trade unions in safeguarding workers' interests and promoting fair labour practices.

Consequently, the Wilson & Others v. United Kingdom case sparked a significant shift in the country's approach to labour laws and employee protection. It highlighted the need for a robust legislative framework that actively discourages employers from penalising employees for their involvement with trade unions. This landmark ruling has been a reference point for subsequent cases involving similar disputes impacting labour rights and relations in the UK and beyond.

**CASE CITATION:** [2002] ECHR 552

**CASE LINK:**

**FURTHER READING:**

**LESSONS LEARNED**

This case was a crucial learning milestone in labour rights. It underscored the importance of protecting trade union members from discrimination or penalty due to their association, reinforcing the principle of freedom of association. The lessons learned from this case led to significant enhancements in the protections provided by UK law. Moreover, the case shed light on the complexities of employment law in the UK, differentiating between various employment categories such as workers, employees, and self-employed contractors. Different categories have distinct rights and protections, crucial for trade union discrimination protection. The case highlighted the need for understanding these categories to guarantee fair treatment.

# HMRC v. STRINGER (2009)

**CASE CITATION:** [2009] UKHL 31

**CASE LINK:**

**FURTHER READING:**

In this landmark ruling, it was determined that workers continue to accrue statutory holiday entitlement during periods of sick leave. The circumstances surrounding this case involved Mr Stringer and his colleagues, who could not work due to long-term sickness.

When their employer denied paid leave, they decided to take legal action. The case was eventually brought before the European Court of Justice (ECJ), which ruled in favour of Mr Stringer and his colleagues.

The Court stated that workers on sick leave continue to accrue leave and have the right to take it at a later date. This ruling also established that workers could carry over their break into the next year if necessary.

Following the ECJ's ruling, European employers were required to reassess their sick leave and holiday entitlements policies. The decision significantly impacted the rights of employees on long-term sick leave, reinforcing their entitlements and ensuring that they are not disadvantaged due to their health conditions. This landmark case set a vital precedent in employment law by ensuring employers cannot deny workers their statutory rights to paid leave, irrespective of their health status. As a result, the Stringer case has been a crucial reference for subsequent cases involving similar disputes over the interplay between sick leave and holiday entitlements.

**LESSONS LEARNED**

The Stringer case served as a significant learning curve for employers and employees. One of the key lessons derived from this case is employers' need to adapt their policies in line with statutory rights, particularly in the context of sick leave and holiday entitlements. It highlighted that the process of accruing holiday entitlements does not cease during sick leave, a fact that employers must now consider. Another crucial takeaway from this case is understanding the nuances of UK law employment categories. The case illuminated how these categories interact with sick leave and holiday entitlements. This case emphasised for employers and employees the importance of recognising distinctions to correctly apply and respect rights.

# AUTOCLENZ LTD v. BELCHER & OTHERS (2011)

This case involved self-employed car valeters, categorised as 'self-employed' in their contracts. However, they contested this categorisation, asserting that they were workers. The Supreme Court concurred with the valeters' viewpoint. The court concluded that the written terms of their contracts did not accurately represent the actual nature of their relationship with Autoclenz.

This case is significant because it highlights the potential discrepancy between what is written in a contract and the practical reality of an employment relationship. It demonstrated that the written agreement might not be the ultimate determining factor for employment status in certain situations. In the Autoclenz case, the judges considered the real-life circumstances and the parties' actions, not just the contract's wording. They found that despite the contractual terms indicating self-employment, the valeters were subject to control and direction from Autoclenz, similar to traditional employees. They were required to follow set procedures, wear uniforms, and could not send someone else to do their work. This underlined that the actual working relationship must reflect the contractual terms for them to be valid.

This case serves as a crucial precedent in employment law, asserting that courts can and will look beyond the surface to determine the true nature of an employment relationship, mainly when there is a power imbalance between the parties.

**CASE CITATION:** [2011] UKSC 41

**CASE LINK:**

**FURTHER READING:**

**LESSONS LEARNED**

This case provides valuable insights into the UK's employment law sphere. The key takeaway from this case is the power of a tribunal to disregard the written terms of a contract if they do not authentically reflect the actual agreement between the parties involved. This means that in assessing the nature of an employment relationship, the practical reality holds more weight than the contract's written terms. This principle is essential when there might be a disparity between a worker's contractual description and working conditions. This case demonstrates that the contract terms cannot simply dictate different employment categories but must reflect the genuine circumstances of the employment.

# BEAR SCOTLAND LTD v. FULTON (2014)

**CASE CITATION:** [2015] ICR 221

**CASE LINK:**

**FURTHER READING:**

In this case, the issue was whether or not non-guaranteed overtime should be factored in when calculating holiday pay. Non-guaranteed overtime refers to additional hours an employee must work, which the employer is not obliged to offer regularly. In this case, the Employment Appeal Tribunal (EAT) was faced with the question of whether the regulation that entitles workers to a week's pay for each week of leave can be interpreted so that payments for non-guaranteed overtime are included in holiday pay. This was a central contention point, particularly since non-guaranteed overtime can form a significant part of an employee's overall compensation. Bear Scotland Ltd, the employer, maintained that non-guaranteed overtime should not be factored in, arguing that it was not part of their employees' regular remuneration.

Nevertheless, the EAT ruled in favour of the employees. It concluded that non-guaranteed overtime should be considered 'normal remuneration' to calculate holiday pay. The EAT emphasised the purpose of paid annual leave to allow the worker to enjoy rest and leisure. The EAT held that this cannot be achieved if the worker is financially disadvantaged during that period. This ruling by the EAT was a landmark decision and significantly influenced how employers calculate holiday pay. The ruling established that workers should be able to take their entitled leave free from financial concerns. As a result, employers were advised to review their overtime policies and ensure that non-guaranteed overtime is factored in when calculating holiday pay.

**LESSONS LEARNED**

This ruling provided an instructive lesson for UK businesses. Before the judgment, including non-guaranteed overtime in holiday pay calculations was not expected. Following the verdict, this led to a significant increase in back pay claims as employees sought to recoup what they believed was rightfully theirs. Importantly, this case clarified the interpretation of the Working Time Regulations 1998. It underscored that 'normal remuneration', including non-guaranteed overtime, should be a factor in calculating holiday pay. This was an essential insight for businesses, emphasising the need to adjust pay policies accordingly. The case underscored fair compensation during leave, supporting a more equitable approach to pay.

# BRITISH GAS TRADING LTD v. LOCK (2016)

The issue was whether commissions should be considered when calculating holiday pay. This situation was close to the circumstances in the Bear Scotland case, where overtime payments were debated. The crux of the matter was to determine whether workers' holiday pay should be limited to their base salary or if it should also include other forms of remuneration like commissions. Both the Court of Justice of the European Union and the Court of Appeal ruled in favour of the worker, confirming that commission payments should indeed be factored into holiday pay. This ruling was a significant milestone in UK employment law, setting a precedent for future worker rights and compensation cases.

Following the landmark ruling in the British Gas Trading Ltd v. Lock case, the implications for employers and employees alike were substantial. For employers, it meant a potential increase in the cost of providing holiday pay as they now had to consider commissions, a component previously overlooked. It signalled a critical shift towards fairer employee compensation, particularly in sectors where commission forms a significant part of their remuneration. It also opened up the possibility for historical claims, where workers could seek adjustments to their holiday pay if it had been calculated without including commissions. This case served as an essential reminder of the evolving nature of employment law and the need for employers and employees to stay abreast of changes to ensure compliance and safeguard rights.

**CASE CITATION:** [2016] IRLR 946

**CASE LINK:**

**FURTHER READING:**

**LESSONS LEARNED**

The cases of British Gas Trading Ltd v. Lock and Bear Scotland v. Fulton have underscored essential lessons for employers and employees in the UK. The primary learning point is recognising the importance of 'normal remuneration' in calculating holiday pay. This includes the worker's base salary and any additional income forms, such as commissions or overtime payments. These cases have compelled employers to reassess and update their employment contracts in line with the evolving dynamics of the workplace, ensuring they accurately reflect the full spectrum of an employee's earnings. This change has enhanced workers' rights, creating a more equitable pay system. It reminds us that employment law should continuously adapt to change.

# UBER BV v. ASLAM (2016)

**CASE CITATION:** [2021] UKSC 5

**CASE LINK:**

**FURTHER READING:**

This case revolved around the increasingly prevalent 'gig economy'. This term describes a labour market heavily influenced by short-term contracts and freelance work instead of traditional, permanent jobs.

This unique case explored the complex relationship between Uber, a multinational ride-hailing company, and its drivers. The drivers contended that they should be considered 'workers' for Uber, contradicting Uber's claim that they were merely independent contractors.

This distinction was necessary, as the term 'worker' under the Employment Rights Act 1996 in the UK implies a person bound by an employment contract or agreed to perform work personally for another party. This party should not be a client or customer of their business. The implications of being defined as a 'worker' are considerable, as it entitles the individual to certain rights that self-employed individuals do not have, such as the national minimum wage and paid holidays.

Therefore, the court's decision in this case would have far-reaching implications, potentially altering how the gig economy functions. If the drivers were classified as 'workers', it would set a precedent that could impact Uber and other companies operating under a similar model. Moreover, it could also lead to significant changes in labour laws, effectively redefining the rights and responsibilities of employers and gig workers in the context of the 21st-century economy.

**LESSONS LEARNED**

This case was a significant learning experience, with the court ruling favouring the drivers. This landmark decision declared that when logged into the Uber app and ready to accept trips within their designated territory, drivers were indeed classified as 'workers' for Uber. This case has set a critical precedent for other businesses in the gig economy, challenging their employment practices and prompting a re-evaluation of how they classify and treat their workforce. It highlighted the need for businesses to examine their workforce relationships, the rights they provide, and the legal framework they operate within. This case highlights the changing employment landscape and the need to adapt laws for the gig economy.

# KING v. THE SASH WINDOW WORKSHOP (2017)

The crux of this case was the classification of Mr King, a commission-only salesperson. The dispute questioned whether Mr King was a 'worker' or an 'independent contractor'.

This distinction is critical in UK employment law as it influences the rights and benefits an individual is entitled to, including holiday pay. The court eventually ruled that Mr King was a 'worker' entitled to a holiday. The European Court of Justice added that if an employer does not provide paid leave, the worker has the right to accumulate their holiday entitlement until they can take a paid vacation or until their employment is terminated. In the wake of the decision, there were significant implications for the UK employment landscape. The ruling set a precedent for similar disputes and initiated a widespread re-evaluation of employment contracts. Companies were urged to reassess their classification of employees, particularly those operating on commission-based contracts or in roles with ambiguous employment status. The potential risk of back-paid holiday claims became a pressing concern for small businesses and multinational corporations.

The case also spurred legislative bodies and unions to call for more precise definitions and regulations surrounding the classification of 'workers' versus 'independent contractors'. The ambiguity of these terms had long been a contentious issue, often leaving those in less traditional employment situations vulnerable. The ECJ statement that unpaid leave could lead to accrued holiday rights triggered an urgent review of policies.

**CASE CITATION:** [2018] ICR 693

**CASE LINK:**

**FURTHER READING:**

**LESSONS LEARNED**

This case has underscored the importance of understanding and upholding workers' rights, particularly concerning paid holiday leave. The lessons learned from this case have led to a significant shift in employment practices and have emphasised employers' need to ensure their policies align with current legal precedents and regulations. These cases have highlighted UK employment law's complexity and nuanced nature, especially regarding the distinctions between different employment categories. Employers and employees must clearly understand these distinctions and the corresponding rights and responsibilities. These cases show the potential outcomes when distinctions are overlooked or ignored.

# DONELIEN v. LIBERATA UK LTD (2018)

**CASE CITATION:** [2018] EWCA Civ 129

**CASE LINK:**

**FURTHER READING:**

## LESSONS LEARNED

The case offered invaluable insights for employers and HR professionals, serving as a guide for handling similar scenarios in the future. It emphasised the indispensable need for employers to take all reasonable steps to gain a comprehensive understanding of an employee's health situation. This could necessitate obtaining medical reports or seeking expert opinions from occupational health professionals. The case further brought to light the importance of individualised treatment of absences. It stressed that each absence should be evaluated on its own merits, considering its unique circumstances. Legal distinctions must be respected, mainly when the absence is caused by illness, disability, or other factors.

This case revolved around Ms Donelien, dismissed by her employer, Liberata UK Ltd, due to consistent short-term absences. The Court of Appeal held that Liberata had made reasonable efforts to understand Ms Donelien's health condition before deciding to dismiss her. This case illustrates the importance of employers taking a proactive role in understanding an employee's health condition. In the subsequent proceedings, the Court of Appeal elaborated on the notion of 'reasonable efforts'. It was stated that Liberata had not just relied on the occupational health report but had taken active steps to understand Ms Donelien's condition. They sought and considered advice from their human resources department, held return-to-work meetings, and gathered additional information from Ms Donelien's general practitioner. Their decision to dismiss Ms Donelien was taken only after these comprehensive measures. This part of the judgment emphasises the necessity of a holistic approach when dealing with employee health conditions and the potential for dismissal.

The Donelien v. Liberata UK Ltd case reminds employers of their employee obligations. It underlines the legal and ethical requirement to fully comprehend an employee's health condition and its impact on their work performance before considering termination. Employers should try all reasonable steps, like seeking expert advice and clear communication before considering dismissal. This case, therefore, is a crucial milestone in promoting employee rights and a more inclusive workplace.

# PIMLICO PLUMBERS LTD v. SMITH (2018)

This case is a prime example of the complexities surrounding employment categorisation within the UK. Mr Smith, a plumber working under contract for Pimlico Plumbers, was initially categorised as an 'independent contractor', a term typically used to denote self-employment.

Being an independent contractor usually means that the individual does not have the same rights and protections as those classified as workers or employees.

However, despite this classification, Mr Smith was bound by certain conditions imposed by Pimlico Plumbers. These included wearing a company uniform, driving a company-branded van, and maintaining a certain number of work hours each week.

When Mr Smith had to reduce his hours due to health issues, his contract was abruptly terminated. This prompted him to challenge the company's decision, citing himself as a 'worker' under UK law and entitled to specific rights and protection against unjust dismissal.

This party should not be a client or customer of their business. The implications of being defined as a 'worker' are considerable, as it entitles the individual to certain rights that self-employed individuals do not have, such as the national minimum wage and paid holidays.

**CASE CITATION:** [2018] UKSC 29

**CASE LINK:**

**FURTHER READING:**

**LESSONS LEARNED**

The Supreme Court's ruling in favour of Mr Smith underscored that the practical nature of an employment relationship takes precedence over contractual labels. This ruling reminded companies that they cannot evade their legal obligations by merely using specific terms in their contract. This landmark case reinforced the importance of the Employment Rights Act 1996. This Act protects workers against unfair dismissal, not just those classified as employees. This case serves as a reminder for companies to consider employment practices carefully and for individuals to understand their rights under UK law, regardless of their employment category, underscoring the importance of correctly applying the distinctions of employment categorisation.

# DUDLEY M.B.C v. WILLETTS (2018)

**CASE CITATION:** [2018] ICR 31

**CASE LINK:**

**FURTHER READING:**

### LESSONS LEARNED

This case is a significant landmark, offering employers profound insights and key learnings. The most critical takeaway is the expanded definition of 'normal remuneration', which now includes the basic salary and regular supplementary payments such as overtime. This necessitates a thorough review and potential overhaul of existing holiday pay practices to ensure full compliance with the law. Incorporating regular voluntary overtime and similar payments into holiday pay calculations is no longer optional but a legal obligation. This move aligns with legal requirements and promotes fairer treatment of employees. This case has transformed holiday pay calculation and expanded the average remuneration concept, promoting inclusivity.

This case revolved around various types of remuneration, including voluntary overtime, standby, call-out work, and travel time linked to overtime. The critical question was whether these elements should be included when calculating holiday pay. In a landmark decision, the Employment Appeal Tribunal ruled that these elements should be included in holiday pay if they are regular enough to be considered 'normal remuneration'.

This essentially means that if these types of work are performed often enough by an employee, they should be factored into their holiday pay. This ruling has set a precedent and is now a guiding principle in similar cases.

In light of the Dudley M.B.C v. Willetts (2018) case, employers are now required to take a broader view of what constitutes 'normal remuneration'. This could include all regular payments, not just base salary.

This ruling has significant implications for businesses, especially those with many employees working overtime regularly. They may now face higher costs due to including these additional payments in holiday pay calculations.

Organisations need to assess their current payroll practices following this ruling to ensure they comply with the law. The verdict is a clear reminder that employment law is dynamic, with court rulings often substantially changing how businesses operate.

# TEST YOURSELF

UK employment law cases encompass a wide array of disputes and legal issues arising in the context of the employer-employee relationship. Among these are disputes relating to unfair dismissal, discrimination based on protected characteristics, and disagreements over pay and benefits.

Unfair dismissal cases involve employees believing they have been let go without a fair reason or following proper procedure. The heart of these cases typically revolves around the employer's ability to justify their actions and abide by correct protocols. The resolutions may result in reinstating or compensating the employee for their loss.

Discrimination cases, regulated by the Equality Act 2010, are another significant area within employment law. These cases occur when employees believe they have been unfairly treated based on age, race, religion, sex, sexual orientation, or other protected characteristics. The outcomes of such cases often involve employers making necessary adjustments to their workplace practices and potentially compensating the affected employee.

Lastly, disputes related to pay and benefits form a substantial part of employment law cases.

**COMPARE YOUR ANSWERS**

Example answers to these questions can be found in Appendix IV on Page 204

1. **How did the Autoclenz Ltd v. Belcher & Others (2011) case redefine the approach to determine worker status?**

2. **How did the Bear Scotland Ltd v. Fulton (2014) case influence the calculation of holiday pay?**

**3. How did the British Gas Trading Ltd v. Lock (2016) case expand holiday pay calculations?**

**4. How did the Donelien v. Liberata UK Ltd (2018) case address the employer's duty regarding disability adjustments?**

**5. What was the implication of the Dudley M.B.C v. Willetts (2018) case on voluntary overtime and holiday pay?**

**6. How did the Wilson & Others v. United Kingdom case impact trade union rights in the UK?**

**7. What was the HMRC v. Stringer case's significant outcome regarding paid leave?**

**8. How did the Uber BV v. Aslam case impact gig economy workers in the UK?**

**9. What critical decision regarding holiday pay was made in the King v. The Sash Window Workshop case?**

**10. How did the Pimlico Plumbers Ltd v. Smith case influence the status of workers in the gig economy?**

# CHAPTER 9
# FUTURE OF EMPLOYMENT LAW IN THE UK

# IMPACT OF BREXIT

The UK's momentous decision to part ways with the European Union, colloquially known as 'Brexit', potentially paves the way for substantial modifications to the nation's employment regulations. As a member of the EU, the UK was obligated to comply with an array of employment laws conceived and instituted at the EU level. These regulations encompassed diverse areas such as work hours, holiday allowances, maternity rights, and safeguards against workplace discrimination.

With Brexit, the UK is technically no longer obligated to follow these EU-prescribed employment laws. This allows the nation to formulate and implement its own employment regulations that better reflect its distinctive social, economic, and political contexts. In essence, the UK now possesses the freedom to shape an employment legal framework that directly addresses the needs and goals of its workforce. However, it is crucial to recognise that the precise nature and extent of potential changes to employment laws remain undetermined at this stage. It still needs to be made clear which segments of employment legislation the UK government intends to amend, retain, or revamp.

Such decisions likely hinge on many factors, including the current state of the UK economy, the necessities of the labour market, and broader political circumstances. Furthermore, it is essential to understand that these potential modifications will not be enacted unilaterally or impulsively. They will be a matter of comprehensive deliberation, debate, and negotiation among diverse stakeholders, comprising government officials, labour unions, employers, legal specialists, and the wider public. This ensures that any alterations to employment laws are just, balanced, and advantageous to all parties involved. Therefore, while the potential for changes in UK employment laws in the post-Brexit era may appear challenging, it also represents an opportunity for the nation to devise a more adaptable and sturdy employment regulatory framework. As a UK citizen, staying updated and participating in these discussions is crucial to grasp how these potential changes may influence your rights and obligations as an employee or employer.

While the prospect of reforming the UK's employment laws post-Brexit opens up the opportunity for the nation to tailor these regulations to its specific needs, it is essential to remember

**DID YOU KNOW?**
Brexit has altered the UK's recognition of professional qualifications. Previously, the UK and EU mutually recognised capabilities, facilitating the mobility of professionals such as doctors and architects. Post-Brexit, this automatic recognition ended, complicating professional employment between the UK and EU. This change, a nuanced but significant impact of Brexit, affects UK professionals' job opportunities and UK businesses' recruitment strategies.

that this is a complex process with potentially far-reaching implications. The nation's lawmakers will need to balance creating an environment that is appealing to businesses and safeguarding the rights and interests of its workforce. The decisions must reflect a thorough understanding of the unique challenges and opportunities the UK's labour market presents.

One area that could see changes is the nature of contractual employment relationships. The UK could move from the EU's model, which has traditionally been more protective of employees, to a more flexible one. However, this would need to be carefully managed to avoid exploitation and ensure fair treatment of employees. Similarly, changes could be made to the rules governing working hours and overtime, giving businesses more flexibility. Still, these changes must ensure workers are well-rested and adequately compensated. Another vital aspect is the impact on international businesses and foreign employees in the UK. Changes to employment laws could affect the ease with which global companies operate in the UK and the rights of their employees. It would be crucial to ensure that the new regulations do not deter foreign investment or make the UK a less attractive place for international talent.

Lastly, any changes to employment laws must be effectively communicated to employers and employees alike. This will require a concerted effort from the government, legal experts, and industry bodies to ensure everyone understands their rights and responsibilities.

# TECHNOLOGICAL ADVANCEMENTS

The rapid pace of technological innovation, especially in fields such as artificial intelligence (AI) and automation, is poised to impact employment laws in the UK substantially.

These cutting-edge technologies are reshaping our work environments, creating new roles unimaginable just a few years ago. For example, the rise of artificial intelligence has paved the way for professions in data analysis and machine learning. At the same time, advancements in automation have led to increased roles such as robotics engineering and automation specialisation. As we progressively integrate these technologies into our workplace, the traditional notion of 'work' is being redefined, causing a shift in the employment landscape.

Considering the pace of technological development, our existing laws will likely need to be reformed and updated to keep pace with these changes. Our current employment laws must be fully equipped to handle these novel roles' unique challenges and situations.

Therefore, ensuring that employees in these emerging industries are protected by comprehensive employment laws that evolve concurrently with these technological advancements is essential. As we navigate these technological transformations, reviewing and updating the existing employment laws is imperative. Such updates could involve defining responsibilities for AI-driven tasks, formulating regulations regarding job security in the face of increasing automation, and establishing laws relating to data privacy and protection in AI-related roles. As a result, the future of employment law must be as adaptable and progressive as the technological innovations it aims to regulate.

The rise of AI and automation raises questions about worker rights and protections. For instance, if an AI system is doing the majority of the decision-making, who is responsible if something goes wrong? Similarly, how do we ensure that job displacement due to automation doesn't increase economic inequality? Our current legal frameworks may need to be fully equipped to answer these pressing questions. It is also vital to consider the ethical implications of these technologies, such as ensuring fairness in AI algorithms and the respectful and appropriate use of robotics in the workplace.

Moreover, the legal system must also be prepared to address these technologies' potential misuse. For instance, there is a risk of AI and automation being used to unfairly reduce labour costs at the expense of workers or infringe upon worker privacy rights. As such, it is not just about updating our employment laws to keep pace with technological change but also about proactively shaping these laws to guide the development and use of technology reasonably and beneficially. This requires ongoing dialogue and collaboration between technologists, legal experts, businesses, and workers to ensure that the future of work is one where technology enhances, rather than undermines, our rights and well-being as workers.

# REMOTE & FLEXIBLE WORKING

The COVID-19 global health crisis has hastened a pre-existing trend: the transition towards remote and flexible working. This modern work style has been swiftly embraced worldwide as a vital response to the pandemic, morphing traditional workplaces into digital domains where workers perform their duties from the safety of their homes.

In the UK, this transition has been particularly significant. The demand for flexible work arrangements has led to a digital migration on an unprecedented scale, fundamentally redefining the traditional concept of a physical office. Instead of the daily commute to work, more UK employees now need to log in from their homes or other preferred locations, capitalising on digital tools and platforms to carry out their tasks efficiently. Nonetheless, this radical shift in our work culture may necessitate a thorough review of our current employment laws. Regulations designed for a traditional, physically present work environment might not be applicable or practical in remote working. For instance, work hours, health and safety guidelines, and data privacy could become more intricate in a remote work setting.

Therefore, these employment laws must be scrutinised and revised to ensure their relevance and efficacy in this rapidly evolving work environment. This could necessitate the creation of new policies to address the specific requirements and challenges posed by remote work or amending existing laws to offer ample protection and rights for both employers and employees in a digital work landscape.

As we venture deeper into this digital age, it is crucial to consider the implications for employee wellbeing. Remote working, while offering flexibility and safety, can blur the lines between professional and personal life, leading to potential burnout. The absence of physical boundaries between work and home can lead to prolonged work hours, as employees may find it difficult to 'switch off'. Also, the lack of in-person interactions can result in feelings of isolation. Hence, employment laws must address these mental health aspects and ensure adequate support mechanisms. The introduction of 'right to disconnect' laws could help maintain a healthy work-life balance. In contrast, virtual team interactions could help foster a sense of community amongst remote workers.

Switching to remote work impacts organisational structuring and management, requiring new leadership styles and team coordination. Labour laws must adapt to these changes, considering fair performance evaluation, promotion, and pay in a remote setting. The virtual workspace's anonymity may result in biases, so laws ensuring transparency, fairness, and equal opportunities must be established. This includes guidelines for objective evaluations, equal pay, and development opportunities in the digital workspace. Our evolving work culture necessitates a progressive legal framework to ensure remote working benefits all participants.

# TEST YOURSELF

The future of employment law in the UK is progressively evolving to adapt to changes in the work landscape, with increased focus on equality, diversity, inclusion, and mental health at work. Brexit has significantly impacted UK employment law as it has led to revisions in immigration policies, affecting the rights of EU citizens and causing uncertainty around the retention of some EU-derived employment laws.

Technological advancements are also affecting UK employment law, primarily through the rise of the gig economy and AI, leading to legal discussions around worker status, rights, and data protection. Lastly, the surge in remote and flexible working due to the pandemic has pushed for legal adaptations to accommodate this new norm, focusing on health and safety obligations for home workers, issues around working time, and the right to disconnect.

In addition, the advancements in automation and robotics are expected to redefine job roles and responsibilities, thereby necessitating alterations in the employment contracts to reflect these changes. Furthermore, the increase in zero-hours contracts and part-time work arrangements is paving the way for more complex employment laws around job security and worker benefits.

**COMPARE YOUR ANSWERS**

Example answers to these questions can be found in Appendix IV on Page 206

1. **What is the potential future of employment law in the UK?**

2. **How has Brexit impacted UK employment law?**

3. **How have technological advancements impacted UK employment law?**

4. **How has remote and flexible working impacted UK employment law?**

5. **What are some of the key legal considerations for employers in the UK with the rise of flexible and remote working?**

7. **How might the advancement of AI and automation impact employment law in the UK?**

6. **What potential changes could Brexit bring to UK employment law in the long run?**

8. **What are the implications of remote working on the employment rights of UK workers?**

**9. How has the UK government responded to the employment law challenges posed by the COVID-19 pandemic?**

**10. How might the rise of the gig economy impact UK employment law?**

technical
investigation, research,
a noncommissioned officer
ranking next above a staff
master sergeant.

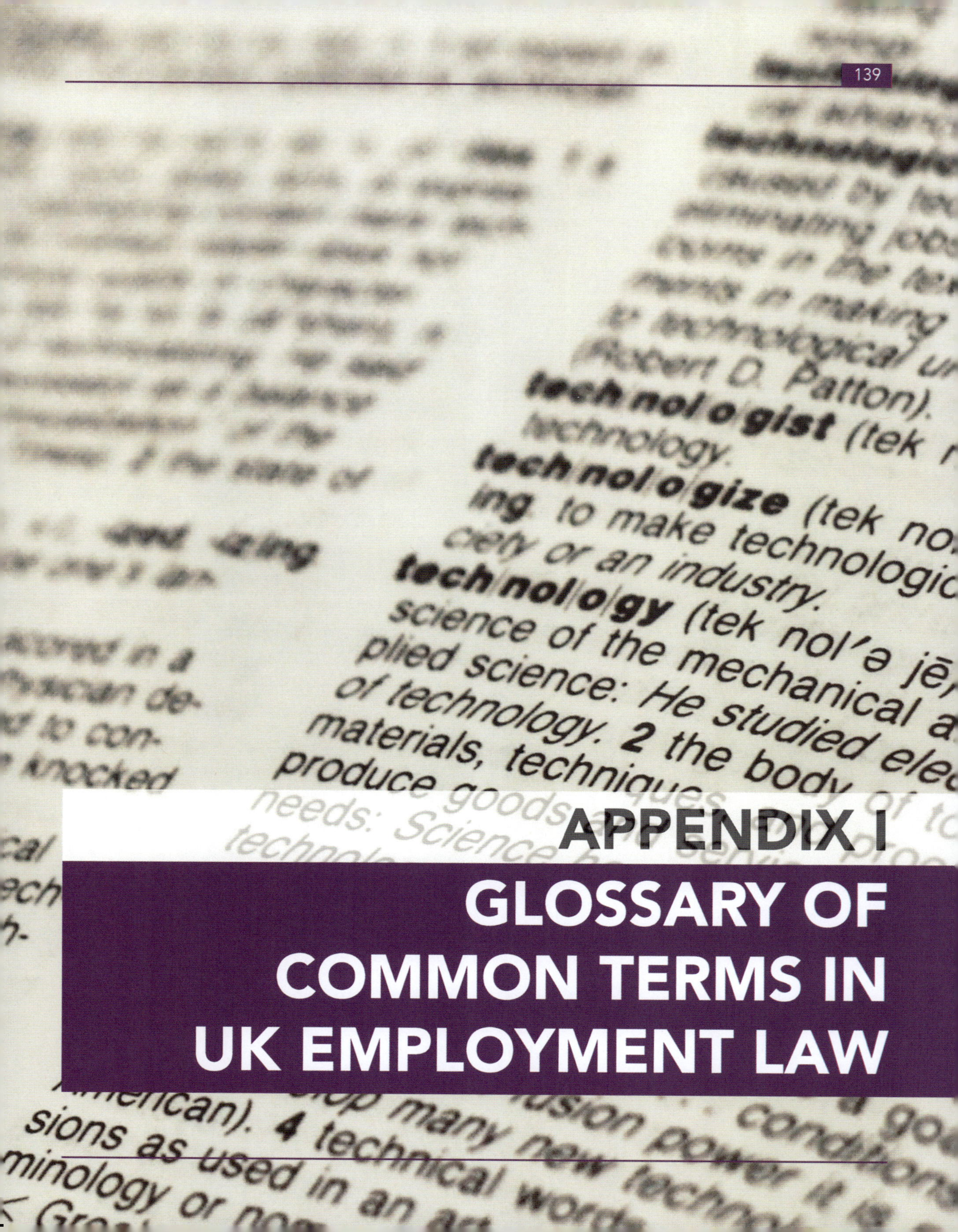


# APPENDIX I

# GLOSSARY OF COMMON TERMS IN UK EMPLOYMENT LAW

# COMMON TERMS IN UK EMPLOYMENT LAW

In employment law, numerous terms are frequently used, and it is essential to understand what they mean. Here is a detailed, coherent, and simplified glossary of standard employment law terms applicable in the UK context.

## A

**Accident Book:**
A legally required document under the Reporting of Injuries, Diseases and Dangerous Occurrences Regulations 2013, in which all workplace injuries must be recorded. This record aids in the investigation and prevention of future accidents.

**Agency Workers:**
These are workers who are contracted via an agency. They have different rights than employees, but after 12 weeks in the same job, they are entitled to equal treatment as if the hirer had directly recruited them.

**Annual Leave:**
Refers to when an employee can be away from work while still being paid their average wage. The statutory annual leave in the UK is 5.6 weeks, which can include bank and public holidays.

**Apprenticeship Agreement:**
A particular type of employment contract which sets out what apprentices will learn, how long the apprenticeship will last and the hours of training. It also specifies the employer's responsibilities to support the apprentice throughout their learning journey.

## B

**Breach of Contract:**
This is when one party does not fulfil the terms set out in the contract. Apart from non-payment of wages or not performing tasks, it can also involve violation of any time in the agreement.

**Brexit:**
Refers to the UK's decision to leave the European Union (EU). This decision was finalised on January 31, 2020, following a public referendum held in June 2016, where the majority of UK voters chose to leave the EU—the transition period, during which the UK and EU negotiated terms of their future relationship, ended on December 31, 2020, marking the official completion of Brexit. The impacts of this decision on various sectors, including employment law, are still being agreed.

**Burden of Proof:**
In legal disputes, such as employment tribunals, the responsibility to provide sufficient evidence usually lies with the employer. This proof supports their claim or defence, for instance, to justify a dismissal.

## C

**Collective Bargaining:**
A process where trade unions negotiate with employers on employees' behalf to determine employment terms and conditions. This can cover various issues, including pay, working hours, and workplace policies.

**Collective Redundancy:**
This occurs when a large number of employees are made redundant at the same time. If an employer makes 20 or more employees redundant within 90 days, they must consult with employee representatives.

**Confidentiality Clause:**
This part of a contract obliges an employee to protect the confidentiality of information about the employer's business. It is also known as a 'non-disclosure agreement' or NDA.

**Conflict of Interest:**
This is a situation where a person or organisation may have multiple interests, and serving one interest could hinder the service of another. It can be personal or professional, and companies must have policies to manage these.

**Constructive Dismissal:**
This occurs when an employee resigns due to their employer's conduct. The conduct must be a severe breach of the employment contract, causing the employee to feel they had no choice but to resign. It is a form of unfair dismissal and can be difficult for an employee to prove in an Employment Tribunal.

**Consultation:**
This is a process where employers and employees (or their representatives) discuss matters at work. It is legally required in redundancy situations and transfers of undertakings, and changing pension arrangements.

**Cover Letter:**
This document is sent with your CV when applying for jobs. It is your chance to explain to an employer why you are the right person for the job and how your skills and experience match what they are looking for.

**Continuity of Service:**
This term refers to the duration an employee has been continuously employed by an employer. It is crucial in determining the employee's entitlement to certain employment rights. For instance, in the UK, an employee's continuity of service is integral in calculating their statutory redundancy pay and eligibility for unfair dismissal claims.

**Contract Rights:**
These are the legally binding entitlements and obligations agreed upon between an employer and employee in their employment contract. It covers working hours, wages, dismissal procedures, and holiday entitlement.

## D

**Data Protection Act (DPA):**
DPA 2018 is the UK's implementation of the GDPR. It is the UK's primary piece of legislation that governs the protection of personal data. The Act has been updated to include the provisions of the UK GDPR while also setting out separate, additional data protection rules for law enforcement, national security, and intelligence purposes.

**Dependent:**
A term refers to someone who relies on the employee for care or financial support, such as a child, spouse, or elderly parent. Employees have certain rights related to time off for dependents in emergencies.

**Detriment:**
Refers to the unfair treatment experienced by an employee due to asserting their statutory rights, raising a grievance, or whistleblowing. It is unlawful for employers to subject their employees to such treatment.

**Direct Discrimination:**
This occurs when someone is treated worse than another person in a similar situation because of a protected characteristic. An example could be an employer refusing to hire a person based on age.

**Disciplinary Actions:**
An employer takes measures to enforce workplace standards and rules. They can range from a verbal reprimand to termination of employment. Disciplinary actions may also encompass written warnings, suspensions, or even legal action, depending on the severity and recurrence of misconduct.

**Discrimination:**
This refers to treating someone less favourably because of specific characteristics, such as age, disability, gender, race, religion, or sexual orientation. Discrimination is illegal under the Equality Act 2010.

**Dismissal:**
This is when an employer ends an employee's employment contract. The release can happen for various reasons, including misconduct, capability or qualifications, redundancy, or a statutory restriction.

**Dress Code:**
This is a set of rules about what employees should wear. The dress code can vary greatly depending on the company, industry, and job role.

**Duty of Care:**
The legal obligation imposed on an employer to ensure their employees' health, safety and well-being. This responsibility includes providing a safe working environment, proper equipment, necessary training, and adherence to health and safety laws.

## E

**Employee Benefits:**
These are non-cash provisions within an employee's employment contract, over and above their salary or wages. Examples include pension schemes, private healthcare, company car, and gym membership.

**Employee Engagement:**
This is a workplace approach designed to ensure that employees are committed to their organisation's goals and values, motivated to contribute to organisational success, and can enhance their well-being.

**Employee Handbook / Staff Handbook:**
A comprehensive document provided by employers to their employees. It details the company's policies, procedures, and practices. It outlines the rights and responsibilities of both the employer and the employee. "Employee Handbook" and "Staff Handbook" can be used interchangeably depending on the company.

**Employee Turnover:**
This measures how many employees leave a company and are replaced in a given period. High turnover can be costly due to recruiting and training new employees. A high turnover rate can also negatively impact the morale and productivity of existing employees and potentially disrupt the continuity of service or operations within an organisation.

**Employers' Liability Insurance:**
This is a mandatory type of insurance for all employers in the UK. It covers businesses against the cost of compensation claims arising from employee illness or injury sustained due to their work for the organisation.

**Employment Appeal Tribunal (EAT):**
This is a tribunal where you can appeal against certain decisions made by an Employment Tribunal, such as those related to unfair dismissal, discrimination, and redundancy payments. Not all decisions are appealable; usually, you can only appeal if you believe there was a legal problem with the original decision.

**Employment Contract:**
A legally binding agreement between an employee and an employer. It outlines the rights and responsibilities, and duties of both parties. This can include details about salary, working hours, job description, and more.

**Employment Practices Liability Insurance:**
This type of insurance covers businesses against claims by workers that their legal rights as company employees have been violated. What is covered can vary depending on the policy.

**Employment Status:**
The classification of a worker's role in a business ('employee', 'worker' or 'self-employed'). Each category has different rights and responsibilities, determined by factors like control over work, financial risk, and obligation to provide and accept employment.

**Employment Tribunal:**
This is an independent tribunal in the UK that makes decisions in legal disputes around employment law, such as claims of unfair dismissal, discrimination, and redundancy payments.

**Equal Opportunities Policy:**
This policy outlines an employer's commitment to equality and diversity in the workplace, ensuring all employees are treated fairly and given the same opportunities.

**Equal Pay:**
This principle, enshrined in the Equality Act 2010, stipulates that men and women performing similar work must receive equal pay.

**Exit Interview:**
This is an interview with an employee leaving the company. It is an opportunity to learn more about why the employee is going and get feedback on the company's practices and procedures.

**Express Terms:**
These terms are expressly mentioned (verbally or in writing) by both parties when the contract is made. They form the basis of the contractual agreement.

## F

**Fixed-Term Contract:**
This employment contract lasts for a certain length of time. It is set in advance, is in writing and states the date when it ends. Upon completion of the term, the contract may either be renewed with mutual agreement, or it will automatically terminate, ending the employment.

**Flexible Working:**
This is a way of working that suits an employee's needs, for example, having relaxed start and finish times or working from home. All employees have the legal right to request flexible working after 26 weeks.

**Freelancers/Contractors:**
These individuals are self-employed or work for a separate business. They provide services for a company but are not part of it. They have different rights and responsibilities compared to employees or workers.

**Full-Time:**
A person contracted to work typically at least 35 hours per week for a specific employer. They are entitled to benefits, including paid leave, sick pay, and parental leave.

**Furlough:**
This is a temporary leave of employees due to special needs of a company or employer, which may be due to economic conditions at the specific employer or in the economy as a whole. It was widely used in the UK during the COVID-19 pandemic when the government paid part of the employees' wages.

## G

**Garden Leave:**
This is a period during which an employee, who is leaving their job, stays away from the workplace or does not have to carry out their regular duties. They continue to be employed and receive their usual pay and benefits. During the garden leave period, the employee is typically prohibited from starting employment with a new employer or engaging in activities that might be a conflict of interest to the current employer.

**General Data Protection Regulation (GDPR):**
A regulation in EU law related to data protection and privacy in the European Union (EU) and the European Economic Area (EEA). It also addresses the transfer of personal data outside of these areas. GDPR can apply to any company worldwide if they process the personal data of EU citizens.

**Grievance Procedure:**
This is a formal process for dealing with employee complaints. It usually involves several stages, including a written statement of grievance, a meeting to discuss the issue and an appeal process. It is intended to provide a fair and transparent mechanism for resolving conflicts or dissatisfaction within the workplace, thereby promoting a positive and harmonious working environment.

**Gross Misconduct:**
This term refers to inappropriate or destructive behaviour that leads to immediate dismissal without notice or pay in lieu of notice (PILON). Examples include theft, physical violence, or severe negligence.

**Gross Salary / Gross Wages:**
An employee's total income before deductions such as taxes, National Insurance contributions, pension contributions, and other employee benefits. The gross salary may include overtime pay, bonuses, and other financial compensations, providing a comprehensive view of the employee's earnings before any withholdings or deductions are made.

## H

**Harassment:**
This refers to unwanted behaviour intended to disturb or upset, typically repetitive or persistent. It is usually related to age, race, religion, sex, or other personal characteristics and can be considered discrimination under the Equality Act 2010.

**Health and Safety Executive (HSE):**
This UK government agency regulates and enforces workplace health, safety and welfare. It also conducts inspections and investigations, provides advice and guidance, and has the authority to prosecute companies and individuals who fail to meet their legal obligations.

**Health and Safety Regulations:**
These are laws and guidelines designed to ensure the safety and well-being of employees in the workplace. Employers have a legal duty to adhere to these regulations.

**Holiday Entitlement:**
This refers to the legal amount of time off work an employee is entitled to each year. In the UK, most workers who work a five-day week are entitled to 28 days of paid annual leave per year.

**Hot Desking:**
This is a flexible working method where employees do not have assigned desks and instead choose where to sit on a first come, first served basis.

**HR Policies:**
These refer to the guidelines set by a company's Human Resources department, covering various employee-related topics from recruitment to workplace ethics. They aim to ensure consistency in employee management, upholding company values, and adhering to legal requirements.

## I

**Implied Terms:**
These terms may not be written down anywhere but are understood to exist in an employment contract. For example, it is an essential term that an employee will not steal from their employer.

**Incapability:**
Refers to a situation where an employee cannot fulfil their job responsibilities due to lack of skills, aptitude, health or any other physical or mental quality. If it impacts business operations, incapability may form a fair reason for dismissal.

**Indirect Discrimination:**
This occurs when a rule or policy applies to everyone but disadvantages a person with a protected characteristic. It is illegal unless the organisation or employer can show a good reason for it.

**Industrial Action:**
This term refers to actions by trade unions or workers when a dispute with employers cannot be resolved through negotiation. It can include strikes, work-to-rule, or go-slows.

## J

**Job Description:**
This document outlines the responsibilities, duties, skills, and qualifications needed for a particular job. It is used in the recruitment process to help attract suitable candidates and can also be used for performance management.

**Job Share:**
This is flexible working where two (or sometimes more) people share the responsibility of a job, including its duties, obligations, and salary. This can allow for a greater work-life balance while benefiting employers through increased coverage.

**Job Specification:**
This is similar to a job description but focuses more on the person than the job itself. It outlines the skills, experience, qualifications, and attributes a person needs to do the job.

## L

**Lone Worker:**
This refers to an employee who works by themselves without close or direct supervision, such as home workers, drivers, construction workers, and agricultural workers. These individuals often face unique safety risks due to their isolated working conditions, and employers must implement specific measures to ensure their safety and well-being.

## M

**Maternity Allowance:**
A financial benefit provided by the government to pregnant women or new mothers who do not qualify for Statutory Maternity Pay. This allowance supports them for up to 39 weeks if they have been employed or self-employed for at least 26 weeks in the 66 weeks before the baby is due.

**Maternity/Paternity Leave:**
These are statutory rights enabling parents to take leave from work for childbirth or child care. Maternity Leave can be up to 52 weeks, with statutory maternity pay for up to 39 weeks. Paternity Leave is typically 1-2 weeks, taken within 56 days of the child's birth. These rights, including pay and duration details, are governed by the Employment Rights Act 1996.

**Minimum Wage:**
This is the lowest amount employers can legally pay their workers per hour. The rate varies depending on the worker's age and whether they are an apprentice. The National Minimum Wage and National Living Wage rates are updated every April by the UK Government.

Failing to meet the minimum wage requirement can result in penalties for employers, including fines and potential prosecution, underlining the importance of compliance with these government-set wage standards.

## N

**Net Pay:**
This is the amount of money an employee takes home after all deductions have been taken off. It is often referred to as 'take-home pay'. The net pay is the amount deposited into the bank account, making it a critical figure for understanding one's income and managing personal expenses.

**Non-Compete Clause:**
This clause in an employment contract prevents an employee from working for a competitor or starting a competing business for a certain period after leaving the company.

**Notice Period:**
This is the length of time that an employee or employer has to give to signal the end of employment. It can be defined in the employment contract, but there are also minimum statutory notice periods.

## O

**Occupational Health:**
This specialist branch of medicine focuses on employees' physical and mental well-being.

**Occupational Pension Scheme:**
This pension scheme provided by an employer can be either contributory (both employer and employee contribute) or non-contributory (only the employer contributes).

**Occupational Sick Pay:**
This is a sick pay scheme set up by an employer which can offer terms more generous than Statutory Sick Pay (SSP). The project's specifics, such as how much is paid and for how long, can vary between employers.

**Overtime:**
This refers to the time that an employee works beyond their regular contracted refers to the time. It is up to the employer whether this is paid or unpaid unless the average pay falls below the national minimum wage.

## P

**Paid Time Off (PTO):**
This is the period an employee is excused from work but still receives regular pay. It includes annual leave, sick leave, personal leave, and public holidays. UK full-time workers are legally entitled to at least 28 days of paid vacation per year.

**Part-Time:**
These are workers who work fewer hours than full-time workers. They have the same rights as full-time workers but on a 'pro-rata' basis.

**Partnership Agreement:**
This business contract outlines the terms of a partnership, detailing aspects like ownership percentages, profit/loss distribution, managerial duties, partnership duration, termination procedures, partner withdrawal or death, and dispute resolution methods.

**Pay in Lieu of Notice (PILON):**
This is a payment made to an employee when their employment is terminated without notice, instead of the employee working through their notice period.

**Pay Scale:**
This system determines how much an employee is paid. Employees' place on the pay scale is usually determined by their experience, skills, and performance. A pay scale often includes defined increments or raises that an employee can expect to receive periodically or as they achieve certain milestones, providing a clear path for salary progression.

**Pay Slip:**
This is a document that an employee receives either before or on payday. It shows how much they have earned and how much has been taken off for taxes and National Insurance.

**Pension Schemes:**
This savings plan helps workers save money for later life. It also has favourable tax treatment compared to other forms of savings.

**Performance Review:**
A performance review measures an employee's job performance and overall contribution to a company. This process helps identify strengths and areas for improvement and aligns individual objectives with the organisation's goals, fostering communication and growth within the workplace.

**Personal Protective Equipment (PPE):**
This equipment will protect the user against workplace health or safety risks. It can include safety helmets, gloves, eye protection, high-visibility clothing and safety footwear. The provision of PPE is generally required by law in many industries, and the employer must ensure everyone has access to and uses the appropriate PPE for their specific job role.

**Pre-employment Checks:**
An employer can conduct background checks on potential employees, such as right-to-work, DBS checks, and references, to verify applicant integrity, assess suitability for the role, and mitigate organisational risks.

**Probationary Period:**
This is a mutually agreed upon time frame, usually at the start of employment, during which an employee's performance is assessed. The length of the period can vary, but it is typically between one and six months. During the probationary period, both parties can evaluate if the employment relationship is a good fit, and it is often easier to terminate the employment contract should either party decide it is not a good fit.

**Protected Characteristics:**
These are the grounds upon which discrimination is unlawful. The Equality Act 2010 lists the protected characteristics as age, disability, gender reassignment, marriage or civil partnership, pregnancy and maternity, race, religion or belief, sex and sexual orientation.

## R

**Real Living Wage:**
A voluntary wage rate set independently by the Living Wage Foundation. It is calculated based on the actual cost of living, ensuring employees can afford a basic but decent standard of living.

**Reasonable Adjustments:**
These are changes or modifications employers must make to prevent employees with disabilities from being disadvantaged in the workplace. Adjustments can include altering working hours, providing specific equipment, or modifying job duties. Other adjustments may involve changing the physical work environment, offering additional training, or implementing flexible working practices to accommodate the needs of employees with disabilities.

**Redundancy:**
This is when an employee's job role ceases to exist, often due to organisational changes, business closure or a reduction in workforce. The law has specific requirements for redundancy, including fair selection processes and consultation periods.

**Redundancy Pay:**
This is payment made to employees who are made redundant, which is based on their length of service, age, and wage at the time of redundancy. It is a statutory right for eligible employees and is designed to ease the financial impact of job loss while they seek new employment opportunities.

**Remote Working:**
This style allows professionals to work outside a traditional office environment. It is based on the concept that work can be done in various places to be executed successfully.

**Rest Periods:**
These are breaks employers are obliged to provide workers during or between work shifts. The standard legal requirement is a 20-minute rest break for every six hours worked and a minimum of 11 hours rest in any 24-hour period.

**Restrictive Covenant:**
These are clauses included in employment contracts to protect an employer's business by restricting the activities of an employee, usually after the employment has ended.

**Retirement:**
This is when an employee ceases to work after reading a certain age or due to health reasons. The UK has a non-default retirement age, so employers cannot force retirement based on age unless objectively justified. Retirement typically initiates the receipt of pension benefits.

**Right of Access:**
A provision under the UK's Data Protection Act of 2018, reinforced by the EU's General Data Protection Regulation (GDPR), allows individuals to make a Subject Access Request (SAR), requesting and obtaining a copy of their personal data held by an organisation or company.

**Right to Erasure:**
Under the Data Protection Act 2018 and GDPR, individuals can request their data be deleted from a company's system unless there's a compelling reason for its processing. This "right to be forgotten" applies only in specific situations.

**Risk Assessment:**
This is an examination of what in the workplace could cause harm to people, to assess whether sufficient precautions have been taken or more should be done to prevent damage.

## S

**Secondment:**
This is a temporary transfer of an employee to another part of the same or a different organisation. The terms and length of the secondment are usually set out in a secondment agreement.

**Self-Employed:**
This is a term for individuals who run their own business and are responsible for its success or failure. Self-employed individuals have different legal rights and responsibilities compared to employees or workers.

**Settlement Agreement:**
This is a legally binding agreement between an employer and employee, which usually provides for a severance payment by the employer in return for the employee's agreement not to pursue any claim in a Tribunal or a Court.

**Severance Pay:**
Employees' compensation when the employer terminates their employment. The amount can depend on various factors, including length of service. This form of payment serves as a financial buffer for the employee during their transition period to new employment and is typically stipulated in the employment contract.

**Sexual Harassment:**
This is unwanted behaviour of a sexual nature which violates a person's dignity, makes them feel intimidated, degraded or humiliated, or creates a hostile or offensive environment.

**Statutory Rights:**
These are legal rights given to all employees and workers by UK law, such as the right to receive the minimum wage, the right to paid holiday, and the right not to be discriminated against.

**Statutory Sick Pay (SSP):**
This type of employee benefits employers must provide to employees who cannot work due to illness.

**Suspension:**
This is a temporary measure taken by an employer, typically while an investigation into misconduct allegations is underway. During a suspension, the employee is still considered employed and should receive their usual pay unless the employment contract specifically allows for an unpaid suspension.

## T

**Tax Credits:**
These are benefits provided by the UK government to support individuals or families with low income. They come in two forms: Child Tax Credit and Working Tax Credit. These credits are designed to reduce the amount of tax owed or, in some cases, provide a refund to the recipient. Tax credits are a vital part of the UK's social security system.

**Trade Union:**
This organisation employees can join aims to protect their interests and improve their working conditions.

**TUPE - Transfer of Undertakings (Protection of Employment) Regulations:**
These regulations protect employees' terms and conditions of employment when a business is transferred from one owner to another.

## U

**UK GDPR:**
A version of the EU GDPR that was integrated into UK law, with some minor changes, after Brexit. It applies the same standards as the GDPR to personal data but with some added provisions and interpretations under UK law. The UK GDPR would apply to any business or organisation operating within the UK or processing the personal data of UK citizens.

**Unfair Dismissal:**
This term refers to when an employee is dismissed from their job in a way that is contrary to the stipulations laid out in the Employment Rights Act 1996. Examples can include dismissing an employee without a fair reason or without following the correct dismissal process.

## V

**Vicarious Liability:**
This is a legal principle where employers can be held responsible for their employee's actions or omissions if they occur during their employment.

**Voluntary Redundancy:**
This is where an employer asks employees if anyone wants to be made redundant. This can happen for various reasons - for example, if the company needs to cut costs or is restructuring. The terms, including severance pay, are usually more generous than compulsory redundancy.

## W

**Whistleblower Protection:**
Legal protections are put in place to protect whistleblowers from retaliation after reporting wrongdoing in their workplace.

**Whistleblowing:**
This is when an employee reports suspected wrongdoing at the workplace. Legal protection for whistleblowers is provided under the Public Interest Disclosure Act 1998.

**Written Statement Employment Particulars:**
This document gives detailed information about an employment contract. In the UK, as of April 2020, this document now needs to be provided to the employee on or before their first day of employment, and it should include key details such as pay, working hours, job title, and holiday entitlement.

**Wrongful Dismissal:**
This is a legal term describing a situation where the employer has terminated an employee's employment contract in a case where the employer had no legal right to do so or did not follow the correct process in the employment contract.

**Work-Life Balance:**
This concept involves balancing work demands with personal interests, family commitments, and leisure activities. This concept involves balancing work demands with personal interests, family commitments, and leisure activities, allowing individuals to effectively manage their time and energy between work and personal life.

**Workforce Agreement:**
This is an agreement between an employer and their workers (or worker representatives like trade unions) about working hours and conditions.

**Working Time Regulations:**
These rules limit the hours that can be worked and provide for rest breaks, rest periods, and annual leave. In the UK, on average, workers can be forced to work up to 48 hours a week.

**Workplace Bullying:**
This refers to repeated, unreasonable actions of individuals (or a group) directed towards an employee (or group of), which are intended to intimidate, degrade, humiliate, or undermine.

## Z

**Zero-Hours Contract:**
This type of contract is where the employer is not obliged to provide any minimum working hours, and the worker is not required to accept any work offered. This offers flexibility but can also lead to unpredictability in income.

# TEST YOURSELF

The tendency to use common terms in UK employment law stems from the need for clarity, consistency, and fairness in the workplace. These universally understood terms help ensure that both employers and employees are on the same page regarding their rights, responsibilities, and the legal implications of their actions.

They serve as a common language, bridging potential knowledge gaps and providing a solid foundation for understanding and applying employment laws. Additionally, these terms facilitate effective communication, dispute resolution, and legal proceedings, contributing to a more transparent and fair employment landscape. Simplifying complex legal concepts into common terms also helps make employment law more accessible to all parties, irrespective of their legal knowledge, allowing everyone to understand their employment rights and obligations.

Common terms in UK employment law also play a pivotal role in formulating employment contracts, as they outline the standards and expectations in a universally accepted language. These terms ensure a level playing field by equipping all parties involved with the necessary knowledge to engage in fair and informed discussions about employment matters.

**COMPARE YOUR ANSWERS**
Example answers to these questions can be found in Appendix IV on Page 208

1. **What does the term "Statutory Rights" mean in UK employment law?**

2. **What does "Unfair Dismissal" mean in the UK employment law context?**

3. **What does "Redundancy" mean per UK employment law?**

4. **How is "Constructive Dismissal" defined in UK employment law?**

**5. What is a "Zero-Hours Contract" in UK employment law?**

**7. Can you explain what "Maternity Leave" is in UK employment law?**

**6. What does "Grievance Procedure" mean in UK employment law?**

**8. What does "Discrimination" mean in the UK employment law context?**

9. **How is "Whistleblowing" defined in UK employment law?**

10. **What is a "Fixed-Term Contract" in UK employment law?**

THE NOVELS OF CHARLES LEVER
THACKERAY'S WORKS
ALL THE YEAR ROUND

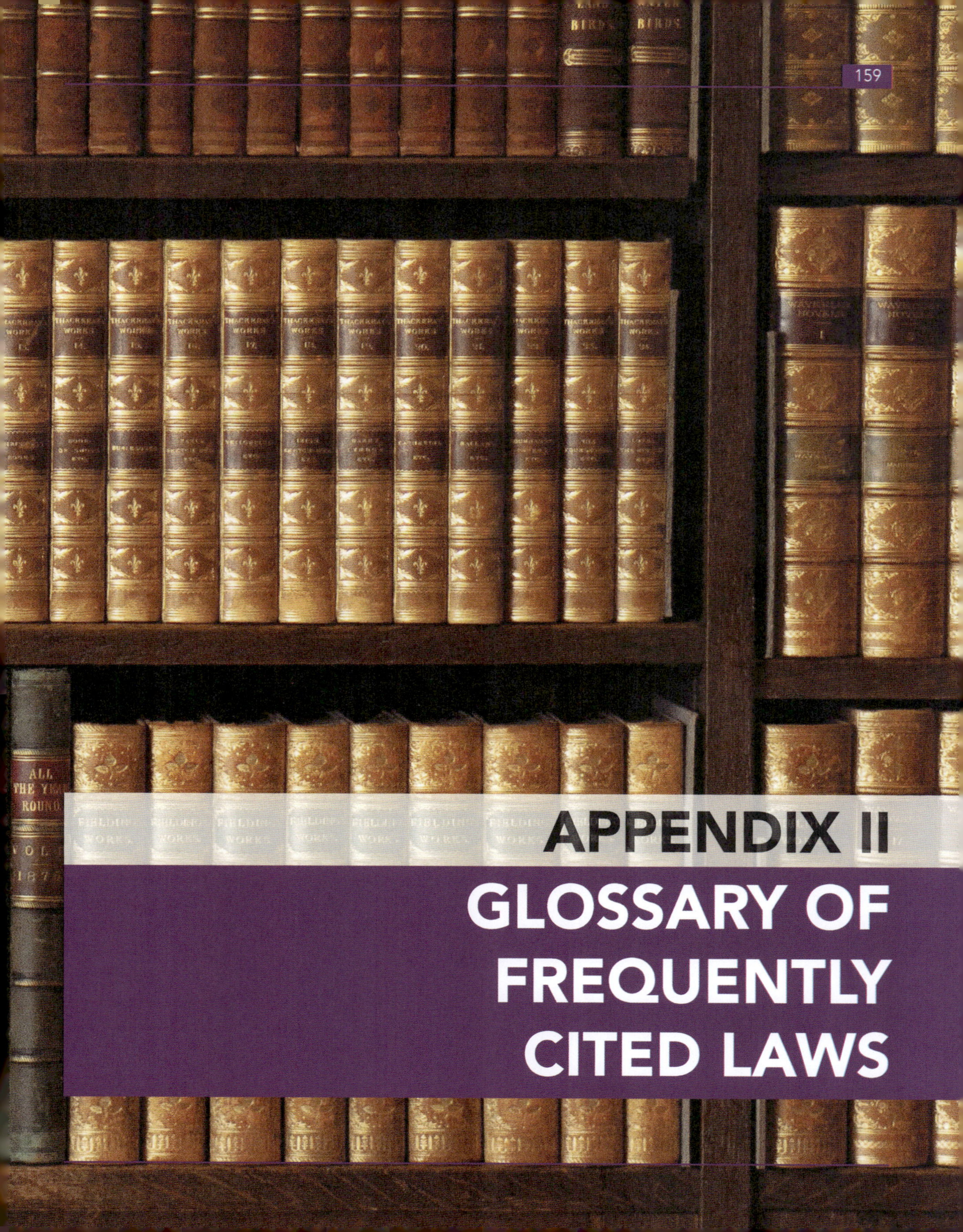

# APPENDIX II
# GLOSSARY OF FREQUENTLY CITED LAWS

# DATA PROTECTION ACT 2018

https://www.legislation.gov.uk/ukpga/2018/12/contents

1. Incorporated and supplemented the EU General Data Protection Regulation (the "GDPR") into UK law. It aims to modernise and strengthen the data protection laws in the UK by giving individuals more control over their data and imposing more obligations and accountability on organisations that process personal data.

2. Sets out the data protection principles, the rights of data subjects, the lawful bases for processing personal data, the conditions for consent, the rules for international transfers of personal data, and the enforcement and sanctions regime in line with the GDPR.

3. Provides for some specific derogations and exemptions from the GDPR, such as for national security, law enforcement, journalism, research, archiving, health, social care, education, employment, and child protection purposes.

4. Established the Information Commissioner's Office as the independent supervisory authority responsible for monitoring and enforcing the Act and the GDPR and providing guidance and advice on data protection issues.

5. The Act enforces strict penalties for non-compliance, including substantial financial liabilities based on an organisation's global turnover. It highlights data privacy by design and default, requiring organisations to consider data protection from the beginning of any project involving personal data. It necessitates the appointment of a Data Protection Officer in certain situations to ensure compliance and transparent reporting to senior management.

   Furthermore, it strengthens individuals' rights to access, port, erase, and rectify the data held by an organisation.

**Amendment I:**
Amended by Data Protection Act 2018 (Amendment of Schedule 2 Exemptions) Regulations 2022 with a new exemption for the processing of personal data to prevent, detect, investigate or prosecute offences related to the misuse of public funds or assets, also modified existing exemption for immigration purposes by imposing additional safeguards and review mechanisms.

**Amendment II:**
Amended by Data Protection, Privacy and Electronic Communications (Amendments etc.) (EU Exit) Regulations 2019 to reflect the UK's status outside the EU by replacing references to the EU GDPR with UK GDPR, also transferred some of the functions and powers of the European Commission and the European Data Protection Board to the UK Secretary of State and the Information Commissioner's Office.

# EQUALITY ACT 2010

https://www.legislation.gov.uk/ukpga/2010/15/contents

1. Consolidated, updated, and supplemented numerous prior Acts and Regulations that formed the basis of anti-discrimination law in mainly England, Scotland, and Wales; some sections also apply to Northern Ireland.

2. Legally protects people from discrimination, harassment, and victimisation in the workplace and broader society based on nine protected characteristics: age, disability, gender reassignment, marriage and civil partnership, pregnancy and maternity, race, religion or belief, sex, and sexual orientation.

3. Imposes a general equality duty on public authorities to have due regard to eliminating discrimination, advancing equality of opportunity, and fostering good relations between different groups when carrying out their activities.

4. Introduced specific duties for public authorities to publish information and set objectives to demonstrate compliance with the general equality duty.

5. Established the Equality and Human Rights Commission as the statutory body responsible for promoting and enforcing the Act and providing guidance and advice on equality and human rights issues.

6. The Act ensures gender pay equality by mandating equal remuneration for similar work, covering salary, bonuses, benefits, and pensions. It also prohibits employers from barring pay discussions, promoting transparency and equality.

7. The Act also establishes a legal structure for positive action to aid disadvantaged or underrepresented individuals with protected characteristics without allowing positive discrimination.

   This ensures opportunities for these groups without infringing others' rights. It empowers Ministers to impose specific duties on certain entities to aid in upholding equality duty.

**Amendment I:**
Amendment pending by Worker Protection (Amendment of Equality Act 2010) Bill 2022-23, to enhance employees' rights not to be harassed at work and extend employer liability for third-party harassment.

**Amendment II:**
Amended by Data Protection Act 2018 (Amendment of Schedule 2 Exemptions) Regulations 2022 with a new exemption for the processing of personal data to prevent, detect, investigate or prosecute offences related to the misuse of public funds or assets, also modified existing exemption for immigration purposes by imposing additional safeguards and review mechanisms.

# WORK AND FAMILIES ACT 2006

https://www.legislation.gov.uk/ukpga/2006/18/contents

1. Extended paid maternity and adoption leave from 26 weeks to 52 weeks for eligible employees.

2. Extended the right to request flexible working to those with caring responsibilities for adults, such as parents, spouses, or partners.

3. Provides statutory maternity pay, maternity allowance, and statutory adoption pay to be extended from 26 weeks to 39 weeks for eligible employees.

4. Introduced additional paternity leave and pay for eligible employees whose partners have a child or adopt a child, which can be taken between 20 weeks and one year after the child's birth or placement.

5. Makes provision for regulations to be made on keeping in touch days, whereby employees on maternity, adoption or paternity leave can work for a limited number of days without losing their entitlements.

6. Further expanded the right to request flexible working hours for parents of children under 18. The Act recognises the balance that must be struck between family responsibilities and work commitments and, therefore, aims to provide greater flexibility in working arrangements for those with dependents.

7. Introduced the provision of statutory shared parental leave and pay. This allows eligible parents to share up to 50 weeks of leave and 37 weeks of pay if their child is born or adopted. This provision gives parents more freedom to decide who will be the primary caregiver and who will maintain their career.

8. The Act also includes a provision for unpaid parental leave. This provision grants eligible employees the right to take up to 18 weeks of leave for each child and adopted child up to their 18th birthday. This provision aims to enable parents to spend more time with their children and strike a better balance between their work and family commitments. This provision seeks to foster an environment that acknowledges the importance of parental presence in the early years of a child's life, promoting healthy child development.

**Amendment I:**
Amended by Children and Families Act 2014 to extend the right to request flexible working to employees with 26-weeks minimum regardless of caring responsibilities.

**Amendment II:**
Amended by Children and Families Act 2014 to replace the additional paternity leave and pay scheme with a shared parental leave and pay scheme, this allows eligible parents to share a maximum of 50 weeks of leave and 37 weeks of pay in the first year after the birth or adoption.

# AGENCY WORKERS REGULATIONS 2010

https://www.legislation.gov.uk/uksi/2010/93/contents/made

1. Aims to combat discrimination against people who work for employment agencies by stating agency workers should be no less favourably treated in pay and working time than their full-time counterparts who undertake the same work.

2. Implemented the EU Directive 2008/104/EC on temporary agency work, establishing a general principle of equal treatment regarding primary working and employment conditions for agency workers.

3. Applies to agency workers contracted by a temporary work agency and supplied to work temporarily for and under the supervision and direction of a hirer, as well as to the agencies and hires involved in the supply of such workers.

4. Provides agency workers with the right to access the hirer's collective facilities and amenities and to be informed of any relevant vacancies from the first day of their assignment.

5. Provides agency workers with the right to the same primary working and employment conditions as if they had been recruited directly by the hirer after completing a 12-week qualifying period in the same role with the same hirer.

6. Regulations require that agencies share comprehensive information with agency workers about their rights, responsibilities, and employment terms and conditions, such as pay, working hours, holiday benefits, and other entitlements. Agencies should also ensure the work environments are safe and fitting for their workers.

7. Employment agencies are regularly audited for regulatory compliance, with non-compliance potentially leading to fines, penalties, and license revocation, while unjustly treated or discriminated workers can seek compensation and corrective measures at an employment tribunal.

**Amendment I:**
A significant amendment to the Agency Workers Regulations 2010 was implemented on April 6, 2020, as part of the Good Work Plan. The notable change was the abolition of the Swedish Derogation model, which had previously allowed agencies to avoid paying agency workers equal pay after a 12-week qualifying period. With this amendment, all agency workers are now entitled to the same pay rate as their permanent counterparts after a 12-week qualifying period, regardless of their contract type. Additionally, from the first day of their assignment, agency workers have the right to access the same facilities as direct recruits and to be informed of job vacancies.

# EMPLOYMENT ACT 2008

https://www.legislation.gov.uk/ukpga/2008/24/contents

1. Reformed a wide range of different provisions of UK labour law, such as dispute resolution, minimum wage enforcement, employment agency standards, and trade union rights.

2. Repealed the statutory dispute resolution procedures introduced by the Employment Act 2002, which required employers and employees to follow specific steps before taking a claim to an employment tribunal and replaced them with a more flexible and less prescriptive system based on the ACAS Code of Practice on Disciplinary and Grievance Procedures.

3. Provides for compensation for financial loss in cases of unlawful underpayment or non-payment of wages, holiday pay, sick pay, or statutory redundancy pay by allowing workers to recover the arrears from the employer or, in some cases, from the Secretary of State.

4. Strengthened the enforcement of the national minimum wage and the employment agency standards by increasing the penalties for non-compliance, extending the powers of the enforcement officers, and allowing workers to bring a claim for unfair dismissal or detriment if they are dismissed or subjected to a penalty for asserting their rights under these standards.

5. Amended the Trade Union and Labour Relations (Consolidation) Act 1992 to confirm with the updated case law on trade unions, in particular, ASLEF v United Kingdom, which held that the right to freedom of association under Article 11 of the European Convention on Human Rights includes the right to trade unions to expel or exclude members on the grounds of their political affiliations.Reformed a wide range of different provisions of UK labour law, such as dispute resolution, minimum wage enforcement, employment agency standards, and trade union rights.

6. The Act also made significant changes to enforcing employment rights. It introduced a new system for resolving employment disputes, under which the Employment Tribunal has the discretion to increase or decrease awards by up to 25% if either party has unreasonably failed to comply with any provision of the ACAS Code of Practice on Disciplinary and Grievance Procedures. This change aimed to encourage better handling of disputes within the workplace, reducing the need for tribunal involvement. Furthermore, the Act reformed the procedure for enforcing tribunal awards and other sums due under employment legislation, making it easier for workers to recover the money they are owed. It also introduced a provision allowing for the 'naming and shaming' of employers who fail to pay tribunal awards, adding a significant deterrent against non-compliance.

**Amendment I:**
Amended by Employment Act 2008 (Commencement No. 3, Transitional Provisions and Savings) Order 2009 by increasing the penalties for non-compliance and giving workers the right to see their pay records.

**Amendment II:**
Amended by Employment Act 2008 (Commencement No. 4, Transitional Provisions and Savings) Order 2009 by giving new powers to the employment agency standards inspectorate to enter premises, inspect records, and issue penalties for breaches of the conduct regulations.

**Amendment III:**
Amended by Employment Act 2008 (Commencement No. 5, Transitional Provisions and Savings) Order 2009 by reforming the employment tribunal system with a new fast-track procedure for simple claims, increasing the maximum costs awards and deposit orders, and allowing tribunals to make recommendations in discrimination cases.

**Amendment IV:**
Amended by Employment Act 2008 (Commencement No. 6, Transitional Provisions and Savings) Order 2009 by repealing and replacing the statutory dispute resolution procedures with a new code of practice and guidance issued by ACAS.

# EMPLOYMENT RELATIONS 1999

https://www.legislation.gov.uk/ukpga/1999/26/contents

1. Made significant amendments in UK labour law to the Trade Union and Labour Relations (Consolidation) Act 1992.

2. Introduced a statutory procedure for trade unions to seek recognition from employers for collective bargaining purposes and for employers to derecognise trade unions, with the involvement of the Central Arbitration Committee as the independent adjudicator.

3. Extends the protection against unfair dismissal and detriment for workers who participate in lawful industrial action, are involved in trade union activities or membership, or use an employment agency's services.

4. Reduced the qualifying period for unfair dismissal claims from two years to one year and increased the limit on the compensatory award from £12,000 to £50,000.

5. Gives workers the right to be accompanied by a trade union representative or a colleague at disciplinary or grievance hearings and to make a complaint to an employment tribunal if this right is denied.

6. Introduced essential changes to the procedures for industrial actions. Trade unions must conduct a secret ballot of members before any such action can occur. The vote must be appropriately supervised, and most members must support the action. Trade unions must also give employers seven days' notice of any proposed action. This measure aimed to ensure that industrial action is a genuine last resort supported by most union members.

7. Established the right for employees to request flexible working. This right can be exercised by any employee who has worked for the same employer for at least 26 weeks. The right extends to requests for changes to the hours, the times they work, and the place they work (as between their home and any of the employer's workplaces). Employers must deal with requests reasonably and can only refuse them for sound business reasons.

8. Enhanced the protections for part-time and fixed-term employees. Part-time workers are given the same contractual rights as full-time workers on a pro-rata basis. Fixed-term employees, meanwhile, can only be treated more favourably than comparable permanent employees if the treatment can be objectively justified. This includes pay and conditions, access to training, and the right to apply for permanent vacancies.

These measures were designed to promote equality in the workplace and ensure that all workers, regardless of their employment status, are treated fairly.

**Amendment I:**
Amended by Enterprise and Regulatory Reform Act 2013 by changing compensatory award limit for unfair dismissal claims to an amount based on the lower of a year's gross pay or existing limit.

**Amendment II:**
Amended by Unfair Dismissal and Statement of Reasons for Dismissal (Variation of Qualifying Period) Order 2012 by increasing the qualifying period from one to two years for employees starting on or after April 2012.

**Amendment III:**
Amended by Work and Families Act 2006 (Section 15) to increase the limit of a week's pay for calculating statutory redundancy payments and the basic award for unfair dismissal from £310 to £330. The limit is now reviewed annually by the Secretary of State.

**Amendment IV:**
Amended by Work and Families Act 2006 (Section 15) to increase the maximum amount of the compensatory award for unfair dismissal from £60,600 to £66,200, the maximum amount now reviewed annually by the Secretary of State.

**Amendment V:**
Amended by Employment Relations Act 2004 by including any reasonable companion.

# EMPLOYMENT RIGHTS ACT 1996

https://www.legislation.gov.uk/ukpga/1996/18/contents

1. Sets out the rights and obligations of employers and employees in various aspects of the employment relationship, such as contracts of employment, wages, working time, holidays, maternity and paternity leave, parental leave, flexible working, redundancy, dismissal, notice, unfair dismissal, wrongful dismissal, constructive dismissal, whistle-blowing, health and safety, and trade union membership.

2. Gives employees the right to receive a written statement of their main terms and conditions of employment within two months of starting work.

3. Defines who is an employee, a worker, or a self-employed person for the Act and clarifies the distinction between these categories.

4. Provided for enforcing the rights and obligations under the Act through various mechanisms, such as complaints to an employment tribunal, claims for breach of contract, criminal sanctions, and civil remedies. Reduced the qualifying period for unfair dismissal claims from two years to one year and increased the limit on the compensatory award from £12,000 to £50,000.

5. The Act also emphasises the right to equal pay for equal work, irrespective of gender. It introduces the concept of "like work", "work rated as equivalent", and "work of equal value", permitting an employee to claim equal pay with a comparator of the opposite sex doing the same or similar job. Employers are mandated to provide a transparent and non-discriminatory pay system. Any breach of this provision can lead to significant financial penalties and reputational damage for the employer.

6. The Act protects against discrimination, harassment, and victimisation in the workplace based on race, sex, pregnancy, marital status, religion or belief, disability, age, or sexual orientation. It introduces the concept of 'protected characteristics', and any unlawful treatment related to these characteristics can result in an employment tribunal claim.

7. Additionally, the Act sets out provisions related to the right to request flexible working. This includes the ability to alter work hours, times of work, or place of work. Employers must consider these requests reasonably and can only deny them for legitimate business reasons. This provision aims to promote a work-life balance and accommodate the workforce's diverse needs.

8. Lastly, the Act lays out the rules and procedures relating to collective redundancies. Employers must consult with employee representatives when proposing to dismiss as redundant 20 or more employees at one establishment within 90 days or less. Failure to comply with these requirements can result in a 'protective award', a compensation payable

to each affected employee. This provision is designed to promote transparency and fairness in the redundancy process.

**Amendment I:**
Amended by Employment Rights Act 1996 (Protection from Detriment in Health and Safety Cases) (Amendment) Order 2021 by extending protection from detriment to all workers leaving or refusing to return to a workplace due to health and safety reasons.

**Amendment II:**
Amended by Employment Act 2002 to include statutory rights to paternity leave, adoption leave, and flexible working requests, and reformed dismissal and grievance procedures.

**Amendment III:**
Amended by Employment Rights (Employment Particulars and Paid Annual Leave) (Amendment) Regulations 2018 to day one entitlement for all workers, enforced since Apr 2020.

# HEALTH AND SAFETY AT WORK ACT 1974

https://www.legislation.gov.uk/ukpga/1974/37/contents

1. Places a general duty on employers to ensure, as is reasonably practicable, the health, safety, and welfare of employees and others at work by providing safe plant and systems of work, safe use and handling of substances, adequate information, instruction, training and supervisions, and a written health and safety policy.

2. Places a general duty on employees to take reasonable care of their health and safety and that of others, to cooperate with their employer and follow the health and safety rules and procedures.

3. Places a general duty on manufacturers, suppliers, designers, and importers of articles and substances for use at work to ensure, as reasonably practicable, they are safe and without health risks when properly used and to provide adequate information and instructions on their safe use, handling, storage, and disposal.

4. Established the Health and Safety Commission and the Health and Safety Executive as the central regulatory bodies for health and safety matters and gives them various powers and functions, such as making regulations and codes of practice, conducting inspection and investigations, issuing notices and directions, and prosecuting and imposing penalties for offences.

5. Provides for enforcing health and safety laws by inspectors, who can enter premises, examine records, take samples, seize evidence, interview persons, and serve improvement and prohibition notices to require remedial action or to stop unsafe activities.

6. Provides for the employment medical advisory service, which offers advice and assistance on occupational health issues, and the medical examination and supervision of workers exposed to specific hazards.

7. Sets out the rights of workers concerning health and safety concerns. This includes the right to refuse to work in conditions perceived as dangerous, the right to be informed of any potential hazards in the workplace, and the right to access training on how to handle these hazards. It also provides for establishing workplace health and safety committees, enabling workers to have a say in their health and safety decisions.

   Furthermore, it imposes obligations on employers to report specific work-related injuries, diseases and dangerous occurrences to the relevant authority, thus ensuring high transparency and accountability in workplace health and safety management.

**Amendment I:**
Amended by Health and Safety (Offences) Act 2008 to increase the maximum penalties for health and safety offences and made imprisonment an option for more violations.

**Amendment II:**
Amended by Health and Safety (Miscellaneous Revocations and Amendments) Regulations 2013 to revoke 12 health and safety regulations and made minor amendments to 16 others.

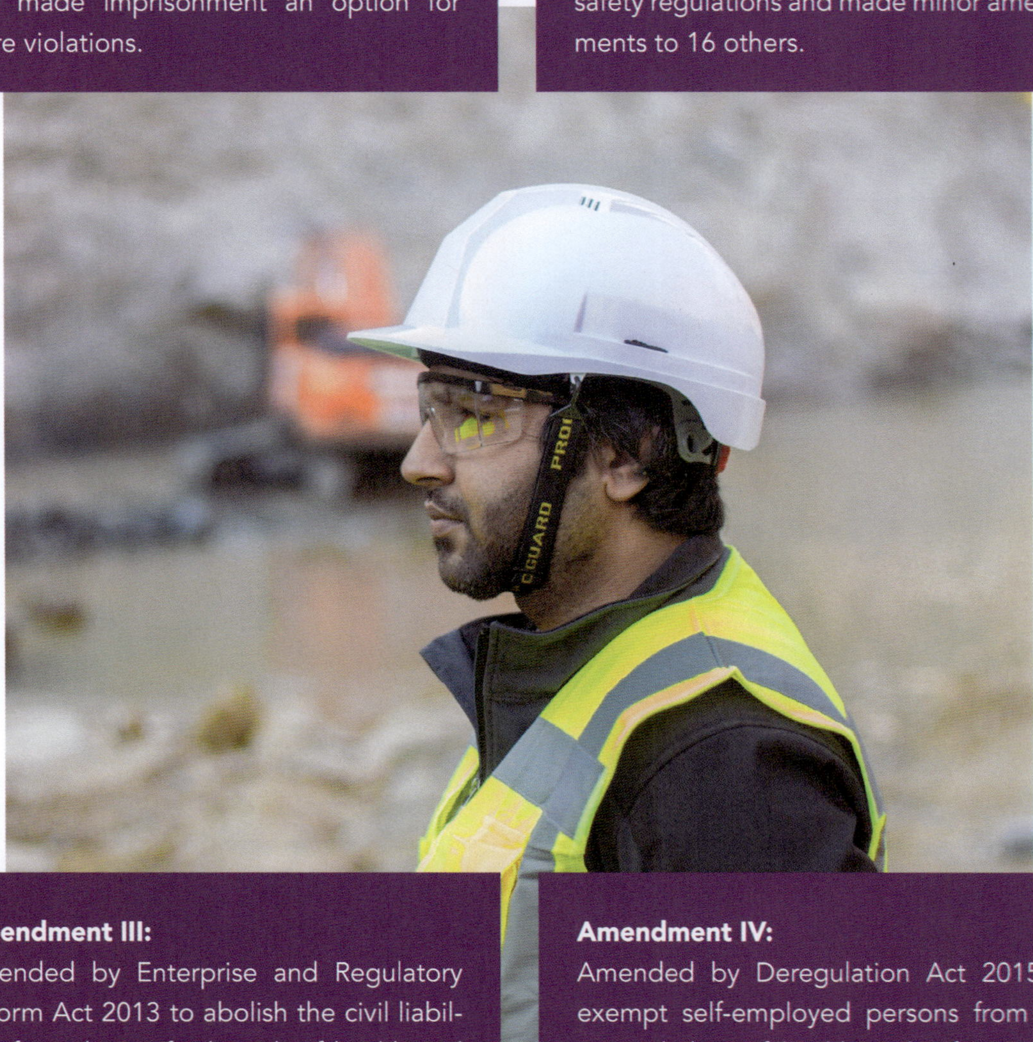

**Amendment III:**
Amended by Enterprise and Regulatory Reform Act 2013 to abolish the civil liability of employers for breach of health and safety regulations, unless the regulations provide otherwise.

**Amendment IV:**
Amended by Deregulation Act 2015 to exempt self-employed persons from the general duty of health and safety unless they conduct undertakings of a prescribed description that may pose a risk to others.

# NATIONAL MINIMUM WAGE ACT 1998

https://www.legislation.gov.uk/ukpga/1998/39/contents

1. Established the Low Pay Commission, an independent body that advises the government on the National Minimum Wage rates for different groups of workers, such as adults, young workers, apprentices, and workers in the agricultural sector.

2. Sets out the basic rules for calculating the minimum wage, including the reference periods, the pay elements, the deductions, and the allowances that are included or excluded from the pay.

3. Defines who is a worker and who is eligible for the minimum wage. It also includes exceptional cases and exemptions for certain workers, such as volunteers, students, seafarers, domestic workers, and share fishermen. Specific exemptions may change over time and should be verified.

4. Provides for enforcing the minimum wage law by the HM Revenue and Customs (HMRC), which can conduct inspections, investigations, audits, interviews, and notices to require compliance, payment of arrears, penalties, and interest from employers who fail to pay the minimum wage.

5. Provides the appeal and review mechanisms for employers and workers dissatisfied with the decisions or actions of the HM Revenue and Customs.

6. Interacts with other laws and regulations, including the Working Time Regulations, the Employment Rights Act, the Equality Act, and the legislatures of Scotland, Wales, and Northern Ireland. This legislation allows workers to claim unfair dismissal or detriment if they face penalties for asserting their rights.

**Amendment I:**
Amended by Employment Act 2002 to include statutory rights to paternity leave, adoption leave, and flexible working requests, and reformed dismissal and grievance procedures.

**Amendment II:**
Amended by National Minimum Wage (Amendment) Regulations 2015 to increase the minimum wage rates for different groups of workers from Apr 2015, also changed the rules for calculating the minimum wage for workers who are paid by the hour, such as salaried workers.

**Amendment III:**
Amended by National Minimum Wage (Amendment) Regulations 2016 to increase the minimum wage rates for different groups of workers from Apr 2016, also introduced a new minimum wage rate, called the national living wage, for workers aged 25 and over.

**Amendment IV:**
Amended by National Minimum Wage (Amendment) Regulations 2018 to increase the minimum wage rates for different groups of workers from Apr 2018, also changed the rules for calculating the minimum wage for workers who are paid by the output, such as piece workers.

**Amendment V:**
Amended by National Minimum Wage (Amendment) Regulations 2020 to increase the minimum wage rates for different groups of workers from Apr 2020, also introduced a new category of workers, those aged 25 and over, entitled to the national living wage.

**Amendment VI:**
Amended by National Minimum Wage (Amendment) Regulations 2021 to increase the minimum wage rates for different groups of workers from Apr 2021, also lowered age threshold for a national living wage from 25 to 23.

# PENSIONS ACT 1995

https://www.legislation.gov.uk/ukpga/1995/26/contents

1. Established the Occupational Pensions Regulatory Authority, the independent regulator of occupational and personal pension schemes, with powers to monitor, investigate, intervene, and enforce compliance with the pension law and regulations.

2. Introduced the Minimum Funding Requirement, defined benefit pension schemes must maintain the minimum level of funding to ensure they meet their liabilities to members and beneficiaries. It also introduced the requirement for regular actuarial valuations and certificates to certify the funding position of the schemes.

3. Sets out the rules and standards for the governance and administration of pension schemes, such as the appointment, qualification, duties, and responsibilities of trustees, managers, actuaries, auditors, and advisers. It also covers the disclosure of information to members and regulators, the maintenance of records and accounts, and the resolution of disputes and complaints.

4. Sets out the rules and rights for the protection and preservation of pension benefits, such as the indexation of pensions in payment and deferred annuities, the revaluation of accrued benefits, the transfer of benefits between schemes, the amount of help on death, divorce or bankruptcy, and the protection from discrimination and unfair dismissal on the grounds of pension membership.

5. Provided for the interaction of the pension law with other laws and regulations, such as the Social Security Act, the Income Tax Act, the Employment Rights Act, the Equality Act, and the devolved legislatures in Scotland, Wales, and Northern Ireland.

6. The Act incorporates provisions for the Pension Protection Fund, a safety net for members of defined benefit pension schemes in case of the employer's insolvency, including levying charges on schemes to fund it. It establishes the Pensions Ombudsman, an independent body to adjudicate pension disputes, and outlines the rights and responsibilities of members, including the right to information and appeal decisions. It also integrates pension law with broader employment and financial legislation, ensuring pensions' consideration within general economic and social policy.

**Amendment I:**
Amended by Pensions Act 2004 which replaced the Occupational Pensions Regulatory Authority with the Pensions Regulator, also established the Pension Protection Fund and the Pensions, Ombudsman.

**Amendment II:**
Amended by Pensions Act 2004 which replaced the Minimum Funding Requirement with a scheme-specific funding regime and a statutory funding objective.

**Amendment III:**
Amended by Pensions Act 2008, which introduced the automatic enrolment of eligible workers into qualifying workplace pension schemes, established the National Employment Savings Trust (NEST), a low-cost, publicly run pension scheme for low to moderate earners, also increased state pension age for both men and women to 66 by 2020, 67 by 2028, and 68 by 2046.

**Amendment IV:**
Amended by Pensions Act 2011 introduced a new single-tier state pension for people reaching state pension age on or after Apr 2016.

**Amendment V:**
Amended by Pensions Act 2017 further increased the state pension age to 68 by 2039 and gave more powers to the Pensions Regulator to tackle pension scams and fraud.

# TRADE UNION ACT 2016

https://www.legislation.gov.uk/ukpga/2016/15/contents

**1.** Implemented a requirement for at least 50% turnout in votes for industrial action by trade unions.

**2.** Stipulated that industrial action in essential public services is only legal if at least 40% of all eligible voters are in favour.

**3.** Introduced a six-month limit for industrial action following the ballot. This limit can be extended to nine months if the union and the employer agree.

**4.** Made it compulsory for the union to provide more detailed information on the voting paper, including information on the voting paper, including a concise summary of the matters in dispute and the planned industrial action.

**5.** Expanded the role of the Certification Officer, the independent regulator of trade unions, and provided them with new investigatory powers.

**6.** Instituted a mandatory cooling-off period of two weeks after the conclusion of industrial action before any further ballots can be conducted. This provision aims to provide the union and employer ample time to negotiate and find resolutions, thereby reducing the likelihood of protracted disputes.

**7.** Included a provision requiring unions to give employers at least 14 days' notice before commencing industrial action, up from the previous requirement of 7 days. This allows businesses more time to prepare contingency plans and mitigate the impact on their operations and services.

**8.** Introduced a requirement for unions to re-ballot their members every four years on whether they wish to continue paying a political levy as part of their membership fee. This provision ensures members have regular opportunities to voice their opinions on their union's political affiliations and contributions.

**9.** Strengthened union members' rights to challenge their union's decisions in court, including decisions about industrial action. This additional protection is designed to guarantee that the rights of individual members are upheld within the collective framework of the union.

**Amendment I:**
The Trade Union (Ballots For Industrial Action) (Electronic Balloting and Miscellaneous Amendments) Regulations 2020 came into effect on 1st March 2020. This allowed trade unions to use electronic balloting in addition to postal balloting for industrial action votes.

# PUBLIC INTEREST DISCLOSURE ACT 1998

https://www.legislation.gov.uk/ukpga/1998/23/contents

1. Protects individuals who make certain disclosures of information "in good faith", also known as whistleblowing, from victimisation by their employer.
2. Allows individuals to bring an action regarding victimisation and claim compensation.
3. Covers various examples of whistleblowing cases, such as reporting concerns about the quality of care, corruption, fraud, child abuse, exam cheating, etc.
4. Applies to workers who make a "protected disclosure" to an employer, legal advisor, minister, prescribed person or body, or in certain other circumstances.
5. A protected disclosure is a disclosure which, in the reasonable belief of the worker making the disclosure, tends to show one or more of

    - That a criminal offence has been committed, is being committed, or is likely to be.
    - That a person has failed, is failing, or is likely to fail to comply with their legal obligations.
    - That a miscarriage of justice has occurred, is occurring, or is likely to occur.
    - That the health or safety of any individual has been, is being, or is likely to be endangered.
    - That the environment has been, is being, or is likely to be damaged.
    - That information tending to show any matter falling within any one of the preceding paragraphs has been, is being, or is likely to be deliberately concealed.

**Amendment I:**
Amended by Enterprise and Regulatory Reform Act 2013 (ERRA) by widening the definition of "worker" to include specific categories of individuals previously excluded from protection, such as NHS doctors, police officers, and students on work placements.

**Amendment II:**
Amended by Enterprise and Regulatory Reform Act 2013 (ERRA) by extending the protection from victimisation to workers subjected to a detriment by co-workers or agents of the employer as a result of making a disclosure, meaning the employer is vicariously liable for the actions of its staff or representatives unless it can show it took reasonable steps to prevent such detriment.

**Amendment III:**
Amended by Enterprise and Regulatory Reform Act 2013 (ERRA) by giving the employment tribunal the power to reduce the compensation awarded to a worker who makes a disclosure not in "good faith" by up to 25%, this is to discourage malicious or dishonest whistleblowing.

**Amendment IV:**
Amended by Enterprise and Regulatory Reform Act 2013 (ERRA) replaced "in good faith" with a requirement that the disclosure be made "in the public interest", meaning the worker must reasonably believe disclosure is in the public interest, not just their interest or for personal gain.

# WORKING TIME REGULATIONS 1998

https://www.legislation.gov.uk/uksi/1998/1833/contents

1. Implementation of the EU Working Time Directive into UK law.

2. Applies to most workers, including part-time, casual, agency, and zero-hours workers, but some exceptions and exemptions exist for specific sectors and professions.

3. Gives workers the following rights:

    - To work no more than an average of 48 hours a week, typically averaged over 17 weeks, unless they voluntarily opt out in writing.
    - To have at least 11 hours of uninterrupted rest a day.
    - To have at least 24-hours of uninterrupted rest a week, or 48-hours in a fortnight.
    - To have a rest break of at least 20-minutes if they work more than six hours a day.
    - To have four-weeks of paid annual leave a year, which can include bank holidays.
    - To have extra protection if they work at night, such as a limit of an average of eight hours of night work in 24-hours, a free health assessment before starting night work, and regular health checks after that.

4. Enforced by the Health and Safety Executive (HSE) and the employment tribunals, workers who are denied their rights can complain to their employer, raise a grievance, or claim to the employment tribunal.

5. The Working Time Regulations 1998 also outlines special considerations for young workers under 18. These individuals are entitled to stricter working time limits, including a prohibition from working more than 40 hours per week and more than 8 hours per day. They are entitled to two days off each week and a daily rest period of at least 12 consecutive hours.

    Employers must ensure that these conditions are met and that working hours do not interfere with young workers' education or training commitments. Non-compliance with these regulations can lead to significant penalties, including fines and legal action from the HSE or employment tribunals.

**Amendment I:**
Amended by Working Time (Amendment) Regulations 2002 which increased the annual leave entitlement from four weeks to 5.6-weeks, including bank holidays, for most workers.

**Amendment II:**
Amended by Working Time (Amendment) Regulations 2003 which implemented the EU Directive on the organisation of the working time of persons performing mobile roads transport activities, such as drivers, crew, and other travelling staff.

**Amendment III:**
Amended by Working Time (Amendment) Regulations 2006 which implemented the EU Directive on the organisation of the working time of seafarers, such as masters, officers, and ratings.

**Amendment VI:**
Amended by Working Time (Amendment) Regulations 2006 which implemented the EU Directive on the organisation of the working time of persons performing mobile and offshore work in the civil aviation sector, such as pilots, cabin crew, and ground staff.

**Amendment V:**
Amended by Working Time (Amendment) Regulations 2009 which clarified the rules on calculating holiday pay, the interaction between sick leave and annual leave, and the carry-over of unused yearly leave.

**Amendment IV:**
Amended by Working Time (Coronavirus) (Amendment) Regulations 2020, which allowed workers to carry over up to four weeks of unused annual leave into the following two leave years.

# TEST YOURSELF

Employment laws in the UK, such as the Employment Rights Act 1996, Equality Act 2010, Working Time Regulations 1998, Health and Safety at Work Act 1974, National Minimum Wage Act 1998, and Trade Union and Labour Relations (Consolidation) Act 1992, are frequently cited due to their broad coverage of fundamental employment relationships. These laws provide a framework for fair workplace practices, aiming to balance employers' and employees' needs and rights. They cover key aspects such as protection against unfair dismissal, discrimination, regulation of working hours, health and safety regulations, minimum wage requirements, and collective rights of employees, making them applicable in a wide range of employment situations.

Additionally, these laws also outline the legal procedures for handling workplace grievances and disputes, thereby ensuring that conflicts are resolved in a fair and just manner. The robustness and comprehensiveness of these laws have made them an essential reference for employers and employees in navigating the complex landscape of labour relations. They serve as a guiding force, instituting a sense of order and clarity amidst the complexities of the working environment and promoting a culture of respect, fairness, and equality in the workplace.

**COMPARE YOUR ANSWERS**

Example answers to these questions can be found in Appendix IV on Page 210

1. **What fundamental rights does the Data Protection Act 2018 provide individuals?**

2. **How does the Equality Act 2010 protect employees from discrimination?**

**3. What are some key provisions of the Work and Families Act 2006?**

**4. How does the Employment Rights Act 1996 protect workers?**

**5. What does the Health and Safety at Work Act 1974 entail for employers?**

**6. What is the purpose of the Agency Workers Regulations 2010?**

**7. How does the Employment Act 2008 support dispute resolution in the workplace?**

**8. What is the significance of the National Minimum Wage Act 1998?**

9. **How does the Public Interest Disclosure Act 1998 protect whistleblowers?**

10. **What is the purpose of the Trade Union Act 2016?**

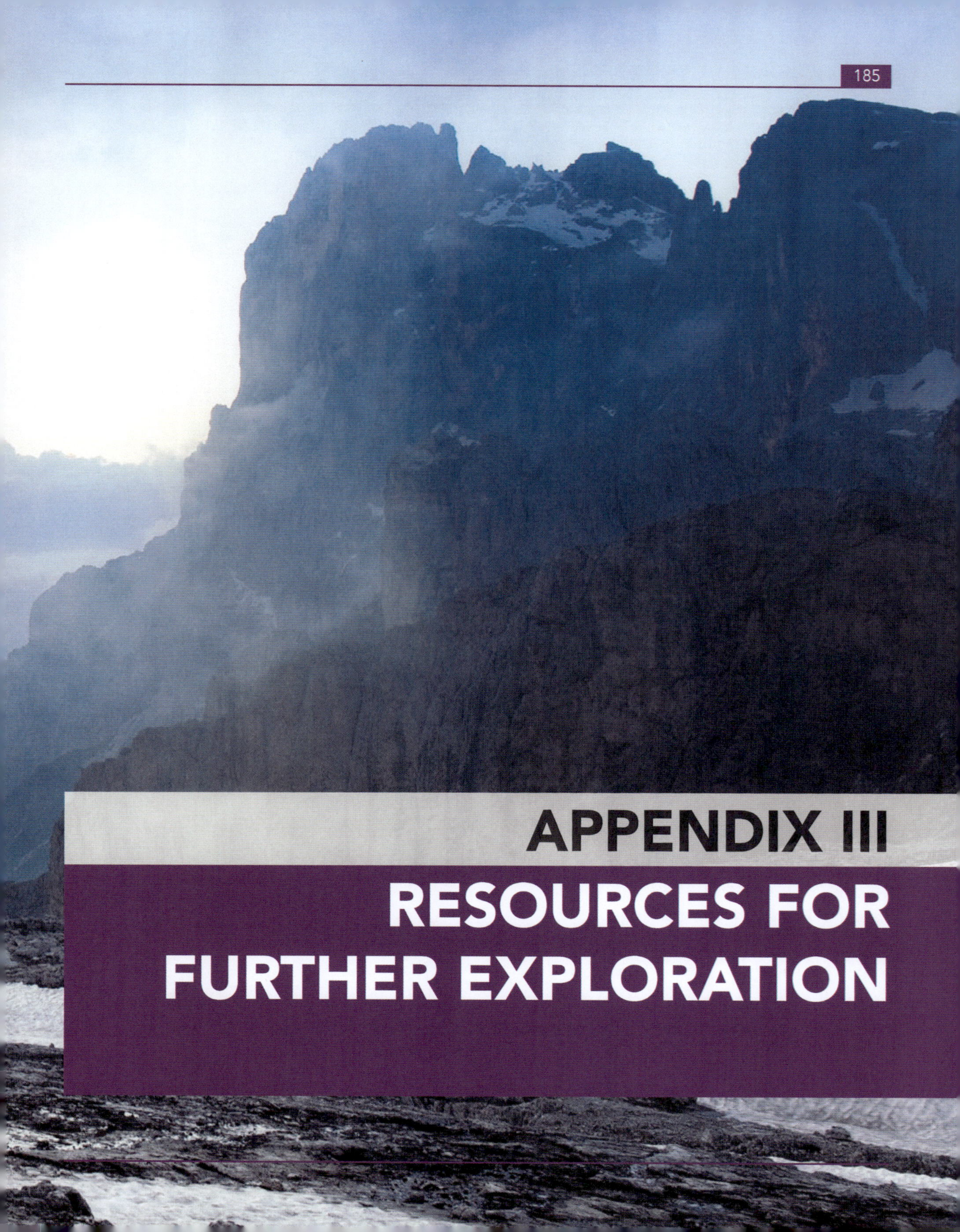

# APPENDIX III
# RESOURCES FOR FURTHER EXPLORATION

# USEFUL RESOURCES

UK employment law is a comprehensive area that covers various aspects of the employer-employee relationship. It includes multiple issues, from employment contracts, working time, minimum wage and discrimination, dismissal, redundancy, and collective labour laws. To delve deeper into this topic, the following resources can be beneficial.

**ACAS (Advisory, Conciliation and Arbitration Service):**
**acas.org.uk**
Offers impartial advice, training, and conflict resolution services to employers and employees to improve workplace relationships and performance.

**British and Irish Legal Information Institute (BAILI):**
**bailii.org**
Provides access to the most comprehensive set of British and Irish primary legal materials freely available online, aiding public legal education and supporting the rule of law and justice.

**CIPD (Chartered Institute of Personnel and Development):**
**cipd.org**
A professional body providing development and certifications, research, advice, and resources for human resources and learning and development professionals.

**Citizens Advice:**
**citizensadvice.org.uk**
A registered charity providing free, confidential and independent advice on many issues, including employment law.

**Croner:**
**croner.co.uk**
A service offering expert HR, employment law, health and safety, and reward management consulting services to help businesses manage their workplace effectively.

**Daniel Barnett:**
**danielbarnett.co.uk**
Daniel Barnett offers an online service that provides expert legal advice and resources, including webinars, articles, and newsletters covering various topics in employment law.

**Employment Cases Update:**
**employmentcasesupdate.co.uk**
An online service that offers comprehensive coverage and summaries of the latest judgments in UK employment law, along with commentary and legal resources for professionals in the field.

**Employment Law Watch:**
**employmentlawwatch.com**
Provides an online service that offers insights, legal updates, and commentary on a broad range of employment law issues.

**Employment Law Solicitors:**
**theemploymentlawsolicitors.co.uk**
An online service provides expert legal advice, representation, and assistance on various employment-related legal issues, from contracts to unfair dismissals and workplace discrimination.

**r/HumanResourcesUK**
**reddit.com/r/HumanResourcesUK**
An independent online community for HR professionals and enthusiasts in the United Kingdom.

**GOV.UK:**
**gov.uk**
The official digital service from the UK government provides access to public services, information on laws and policies, and general guidance on a wide range of topics, all in one place.

**ICO (Information Commissioner's Office):**
**ico.org.uk**
The autonomous authority for upholding information rights in the public interest in the United Kingdom. The ICO is committed to promoting and enforcing data protection laws, providing resources and guidance to businesses and individuals while safeguarding personal data rights.

**The Law Society:**
**lawsociety.org.uk**
The independent professional body for solicitors in England and Wales, providing support and guidance to practitioners while upholding the rule of law and safeguarding the rights of individuals.

**Lexology:**
**lexology.com**
An innovative online service that provides global legal updates, analysis, and insights from leading law firms, helping professionals stay on top of current trends and changes in law that matter to their business.

**New Law Journal:**
**newlawjournal.co.uk**
Offers an online service that provides in-depth legal analysis, news, expert commentary, and case reports across all areas of law, keeping legal professionals updated with the latest developments and trends.

**Parliamentary Bills UK:**
**bills.parliament.uk**
Provides online information about proposed laws (bills) in the UK Parliament, tracking their progress, detailing their contents, and offering updates on their amendments and debates.

**UK Labour Law Blog:**
**uklabourlawblog.com**
An online platform that provides critical commentary and analysis on current employment and labour law issues, offering insights from various legal experts and practitioners.

**XpertHR:**
**xperthr.co.uk**
A comprehensive online service providing HR professionals with the resources they need to comply with employment law and best practices.

# APPENDIX IV
# TEST YOURSELF - THE ANSWERS

# TEST YOURSELF ANSWERS - CHAPTER 1

1. **Under UK employment law, what types of discrimination are prohibited in the workplace?**
The UK's Equality Act 2010 prohibits discrimination based on nine protected characteristics: age, disability, gender reassignment, marriage and civil partnership, pregnancy and maternity, race, religion or belief, sex, and sexual orientation. This applies to all aspects of employment, including recruitment, terms and conditions, promotions, transfers, dismissals, and training.

2. **What are some of an employer's critical responsibilities regarding Health and Safety in the workplace?**
Under the Health and Safety at Work Act 1974, employers are responsible for ensuring the welfare of their employees in the workplace. This includes conducting risk assessments, implementing safety measures, providing adequate training and supervision, maintaining safe and healthy working conditions, and ensuring machinery and equipment are safe to use.

3. **What is the difference between fair and unfair dismissal?**
Fair dismissal occurs when an employer has a valid reason for terminating an employee's contract and follows the correct procedure. The right reasons can include redundancy, misconduct, or capability. Unfair dismissal occurs when an employer does not have a good reason for the dismissal or fails to follow the correct procedure.

4. **How does UK employment law protect employee data?**
Under the Data Protection Act 2018, which incorporates the EU's General Data Protection Regulation (GDPR), employers must protect the personal data of their employees. This means they have to keep the data secure, not disclose it unlawfully, and only use it for specified legitimate purposes. Employees also have the right to access their data and correct any inaccuracies.

5. **What are the different types of employment contracts?**
UK employment law recognises various types of employment contracts, including permanent full-time contracts, part-time contracts, fixed-term contracts, and zero-hour contracts. Each contract type has different implications for job security, working hours, and benefits.

6. **How does UK employment law define the scope of 'employee' and 'worker'?**
In UK employment law, 'employees' are individuals who work under a contract of employment and have the most employment rights. 'Workers', on the other hand, have a contract to do work or services and have some employment rights such as receiving the National Minimum Wage and statutory minimum holiday

7. **Can UK employers change an employment contract without an employee's consent?**
Generally, an employer can only change an employee's contract with their agreement. Changes should be agreed upon between both parties. If the employer imposes changes without the employee's agreement, it could lead to a breach of contract.

8. **What rights does an employee have if made redundant in the UK?**
If an employee is made redundant, they may have the right to redundancy pay, a notice period, consultation with their employer, the option to move into a different job, and time off to find a new job, depending on their circumstances and length of service.

9. **What are the consequences for an employer if they fail to adhere to health and safety regulations?**
If an employer fails to meet health and safety regulations, they could face severe penalties, including fines, imprisonment, or both. They may also be sued for personal injury by the employee.

10. **How does UK employment law ensure equal pay for men and women?**
The UK's Equality Act 2010 stipulates that men and women in the same employment performing equal work must receive equal pay. This covers not just wages but also all other contractual terms and conditions of employment, such as holiday entitlement, bonuses, pay and reward schemes, pension payments and other benefits.

**COMPARE YOUR ANSWERS**
These answers are for the questions at the end of Chapter 1 on pages 28-31.

# TEST YOURSELF ANSWERS - CHAPTER 2

1. **What fundamental rights are every employee entitled to?**
Every employee in the UK is entitled to a minimum wage, a safe working environment, protection against unlawful discrimination, statutory holiday and sick pay, and the right to join a trade union, among other rights.

2. **What does "Right of Access" mean in the employment law context?**
The "Right of Access," also known as Subject Access Request (SAR), under the General Data Protection Regulation (GDPR), allows employees to request access to the personal data that the employer holds about them.

3. **What is the "Right to Erasure" in the employment law context?**
The "Right to Erasure," also known as the "right to be forgotten," is a principle under GDPR that allows an individual to request the deletion or removal of personal data where there is no compelling reason for its continued processing.

4. **What are some key responsibilities of employers?**
Key responsibilities of employers in the UK include providing a safe and healthy working environment, paying employees on time, treating employees fairly and without discrimination, respecting employees' rights under employment law, and ensuring data protection.

5. **In the employment law context, what is the "Imperative of Equality"?**
The "Imperative of Equality" in UK employment law refers to the requirement for employers to treat all employees equally and not discriminate against them based on protected characteristics such as race, age, gender, disability, religion or belief, and sexual orientation.

6. **What is the process for an employee to raise a grievance?**
If an employee has a complaint (a grievance) at work, it's usually a good idea for them to first speak to their employer informally. If this doesn't resolve the issue, the employee can formally raise it in writing to their employer. This is known as submitting a formal grievance.

**7. What are the exceptions to the "Right to Erasure"?**

The "Right to Erasure" does not apply if processing is necessary for one of the following reasons: to exercise the right of freedom of expression and information, to comply with a legal obligation, for the performance of a task carried out in the public interest or in the exercise of official authority, for archiving purposes in the public interest, scientific research historical research or statistical purposes where erasure is likely to render impossible or seriously impair the achievement of that processing, or for the establishment, exercise or defence of legal claims.

**8. What responsibilities do employers have regarding employee training?**

Employers are required to ensure their employees are suitably trained to carry out their jobs safely. This could be through providing on-the-job training, sending employees on courses, or providing adequate supervision.

**9. How does TUPE protect an employee's rights during a business transfer?**

TUPE protects employees' rights when the business they work for, or part of it, is sold or transferred to a new employer. It involves the automatic transfer of employees and any liabilities associated with them from the old employer to the new employer.

**10. How can employers demonstrate their commitment to the imperative of equality?**

Employers can demonstrate their commitment to equality in various ways. This can include developing and enforcing a solid equal opportunities policy, providing employee equality and diversity training, promoting an inclusive and respectful work culture, and taking prompt action against discriminatory behaviour.

**COMPARE YOUR ANSWERS**

These answers are for the questions at the end of Chapter 2 on pages 46-49.

# TEST YOURSELF ANSWERS - CHAPTER 3

1. **What is an Employment Contract, and why is it significant in the UK?**
An employment contract is a written legal document laying out binding employment terms and conditions between an employee and an employer. It is significant in the UK because it safeguards both the employer's and employee's rights and can serve as a reference point if disputes arise in the future. It also provides clarity on job roles, responsibilities, and expectations.

2. **What key elements must be included in an Employment Contract?**
Key elements of an Employment Contract typically include the name of the employer and employee, job description, date of commencement of employment, salary details, working hours, holiday entitlement, sick pay rules, notice period for termination, and grievance procedures.

3. **What rights do employees have under an Employment Contract in the UK?**
Employees have the right to receive the National Minimum Wage, the right to not work more than 48 hours on average per week or to opt out of this right if they choose, the right to paid holiday, the right not to be unfairly dismissed, and the right to receive a redundancy payment if made redundant.

4. **Are there any industry-specific rights that employees should know?**
Yes, some industries have specific rights for their employees. For example, typical health and safety regulations exist in the construction industry. The healthcare sector has particular rules about working hours and mandatory breaks. Employees must familiarise themselves with the rights specific to their industry.

5. **Can the terms of an Employment Contract be changed after it has been signed?**
Generally, the terms of an Employment Contract can only be changed with agreement from both the employer and employee. Suppose an employer wants to make changes to the contract. In that case, they must notify the employee and obtain their consent. Suppose an employee disagrees with the changes. In that case, they may have the right to refuse to work under the changed conditions or may even have a claim for unfair dismissal.

6. **What happens if an employer breaches the terms of an Employment Contract in the UK?**
In the UK, if an employer breaches the terms of the Employment Contract, the employee may resign and claim constructive dismissal. However, this is a complicated area of law, and it is advised that the employee seek legal advice before making such a decision.

7. **Does an Employment Contract need to be written and signed to be valid in the UK?**
A written contract is only sometimes obligatory in the UK but is highly recommended. Whether the contract is verbal, written, or a mix of both, the employee has a legal right to a written statement outlining the main terms of their agreement within two months of starting work.

8. **What steps should an employee take if they have not received a written contract within two months of starting work?**
UK employment law mandates that an employee receive a written statement of the main terms of the agreement within two months of starting work. If this has not happened, the employee should request this from their employer first. If the employer fails to provide it, the employee can seek help from an employment tribunal or a legal professional..

9. **Can an employee work for another employer under an Employment Contract?**
The ability of an employee to work for another employer is contingent on the terms of their Employment Contract. Some contracts include an 'exclusivity clause' prohibiting an employee from working for another employer. However, it's important to note that exclusivity clauses in zero-hours contracts are illegal in the UK.

10. **How are Employment Contracts handled in the case of business mergers or takeovers in the UK?**
In the event of business mergers or takeovers in the UK, the Transfer of Undertakings (Protection of Employment) regulations, known as TUPE, protect the employment contracts of the employees. With these regulations, the new employer assumes the employees' contracts without altering the terms and conditions. Employees retain their service continuity, and employers must follow the correct procedure, including informing and consulting employees about the transfer.

**COMPARE YOUR ANSWERS**

These answers are for the questions at the end of Chapter 3 on pages 60-63.

# TEST YOURSELF ANSWERS - CHAPTER 4

1. **What is the current (2023) National Minimum Wage for individuals aged 23 and over in the UK?**
   As of April 2023, the National Living Wage (the minimum wage for people aged 23 and over) is £10.42 per hour.

2. **How has the National Minimum Wage in the UK evolved over the years?**
   The National Minimum Wage was introduced in the UK in 1999 at a rate of £3.60 for adults. Since then, it has steadily increased, reflecting economic conditions and the cost of living. In 2016, the government introduced a higher minimum wage rate for all staff over 25, initially set at £7.20—the National Living Wage.

3. **Under UK employment law, are employers always required to pay their employees extra for overtime work?**
   Not necessarily. Whether or not an employee is entitled to overtime, pay will depend on their specific employment contract. Some contracts state that employees are entitled to 'time-and-a-half' or 'double time' for overtime. Still, there is only a legal requirement for this in the UK if the average pay falls below the National Minimum Wage.

4. **How does holiday pay work in the UK?**
   Full-time employees in the UK are entitled to a minimum of 5.6 weeks (28 days) of paid holiday per year, including public holidays. Part-time workers are entitled to the same level of holiday pro rata. The amount of pay that the worker receives is based on a 'week's pay' for each week of leave.

5. **What are the employer's responsibilities concerning workplace pensions in the UK?**
   Under the UK employment law, employers must automatically enrol employees into a pension scheme if they are between 22 and State Pension age, earn at least £10,000 a year, and work in the UK. Employers are also required to make minimum contributions to the pension scheme. The total minimum contribution is currently set at 8% of qualifying earnings, of which a minimum of 3% must come from the employer, with the employee making up the difference.

6. **Are apprentices eligible for the UK National Minimum Wage?**
Yes, apprentices are eligible for the National Minimum Wage. However, the rate is lower than that for other workers. As of April 2023, the minimum wage for apprentices is £5.28 per hour. This rate applies to apprentices under 18 and those aged 19 or over in their first year of apprenticeship.

7. **How often is the National Minimum Wage revised in the UK?**
The National Minimum Wage rates are usually reviewed and updated annually in April by the government, based on the recommendations of the Low Pay Commission.

8. **Are part-time workers in the UK entitled to the same benefits as full-time workers?**
Yes, part-time workers have the same employment rights as full-time workers on a pro-rata basis. This includes the right to the National Minimum Wage, paid holiday, and access to a workplace pension scheme.

9. **If employees work on a public holiday, are they entitled to extra pay under UK employment law?**
There is no legal right to pay for working on a public holiday or extra pay if public holidays are worked. Some employers, however, offer higher pay for workers who work on these days as part of their employment contract.

10. **What happens if an employer does not comply with the legal requirements for pensions in the UK?**
Employers who do not comply with their duties for automatic enrolment into a workplace pension scheme may face enforcement action from The Pensions Regulator. This can range from warning letters and statutory notices to penalty notices and court action.

**COMPARE YOUR ANSWERS**
These answers are for the questions at the end of Chapter 4 on pages 74-77.

# TEST YOURSELF ANSWERS - CHAPTER 5

1. **What are the primary responsibilities of an employer regarding health and safety in the workplace?**
The primary responsibilities of an employer concerning health and safety in the workplace include providing a safe and healthy working environment, ensuring all machinery and equipment are safe, and ensuring that safe working practices are set up and followed. They are also responsible for providing adequate first aid facilities, giving workers information and training on health and safety, and reporting certain accidents, injuries, diseases, and dangerous occurrences to the relevant authority.

2. **What rights do employees have concerning health and safety in the workplace?**
Employees have the right to work in environments where risks to their health and safety are adequately controlled. They also have the right to stop work and leave their work area without fear of disciplinary action if they have reasonable concerns about their safety. Furthermore, they have the right to be consulted by their employer on health and safety issues.

3. **What is an employer's duty in case of a workplace accident?**
In the event of a workplace accident, employers are required by UK law to report certain types of injuries, diseases, and dangerous occurrences. This is usually done through the Reporting of Injuries, Diseases, and Dangerous Occurrences Regulations (RIDDOR). Employers also have to provide first aid equipment and facilities and ensure employees receive immediate attention if injured or taken ill at work.

4. **How can employers effectively reduce the risk of workplace illnesses?**
Employers can reduce the risk of workplace illnesses by implementing a health and safety policy, conducting risk assessments, providing adequate training and information about potential hazards, ensuring good hygiene practices, providing protective clothing and equipment where necessary, and regularly monitoring and reviewing the working environment.

5. **What steps should employers take to fulfil their health and safety obligations?**
Employers should conduct regular risk assessments to identify potential hazards, implement measures to control these risks, and communicate this information to all employees. They should also provide adequate training on health and

safety, ensure the workplace and equipment are maintained to a safe standard, have a straightforward emergency procedure in place, and regularly review and update their health and safety policies and procedures.

6. **Can employees refuse to work if they believe their workplace is unsafe?**
Yes, under UK employment law, if an employee reasonably believes there is a serious and imminent danger to their health and safety, they have the right to leave their workplace or refuse to return while the risk persists.

7. **What other obligations does an employer have regarding health and safety?**
Employers must also provide information, instruction, training, and supervision for health and safety. They must ensure that suitable and sufficient risk assessments are carried out and that the necessary health surveillance is provided.

8. **What should an employer do if a worker becomes ill because of their work?**
If a worker becomes ill due to their work, the employer should report the illness to the relevant authority if it is reportable under RIDDOR. The employer should also review their risk assessment and consider whether additional measures must be taken to prevent the illness from recurring.

9. **Is it an employer's responsibility to provide employees personal protective equipment (PPE)?**
Yes, under the Personal Protective Equipment at Work Regulations 1992, employers must provide suitable PPE to employees who may be exposed to a risk to their health and safety while at work unless the threat has been adequately controlled by other means.

10. **What are the potential consequences for an employer if they fail to comply with health and safety regulations?**
If an employer fails to comply with health and safety regulations, they could face enforcement action from the Health and Safety Executive (HSE) or local authority. This could include improvement or prohibition notices, fines, or even prosecution. Furthermore, they could be held liable for any harm caused to employees or others due to non-compliance.

**COMPARE YOUR ANSWERS**

These answers are for the questions at the end of Chapter 5 on pages 84-87.

# TEST YOURSELF ANSWERS - CHAPTER 6

1. **According to UK employment law, what is the first step to take if an issue arises in the workplace?**
The first step generally involves conversing or meeting with the parties involved to understand and discuss the issue. Applying a line manager or HR in this initial discussion is often recommended. Suppose the problem cannot be resolved informally. Moving on to a formal procedure, such as raising a grievance, may be necessary in that case.

2. **What is one of the UK's most common employment law issues?**
One of the most common issues pertains to unfair dismissal claims. This arises when an employee believes they have been dismissed from their job without a fair reason or the employer did not follow the correct procedure.

3. **How important is communication and negotiation in resolving workplace disputes?**
Communication and negotiation are vital in resolving workplace disputes. Clear, open, and respectful communication can prevent misunderstandings and resolve issues before they escalate. Negotiation can lead to compromises that satisfy all parties involved.

4. **What is the role of mediation in employment issues?**
Mediation is a voluntary process where a neutral third party helps the disputing parties to reach a mutually acceptable solution. It can be an effective way of resolving disputes without formal procedures or legal action. Mediation can save time, reduce stress, and maintain or even improve working relationships.

5. **How does conciliation differ from mediation in employment law?**
Both conciliation and mediation involve a neutral third party assisting disputing parties to reach a resolution. However, conciliation usually involves the conciliator proposing solutions and playing a more active role in finding a resolution. At the same time, a mediator primarily facilitates communication between the parties and helps them generate their own solutions. In the UK, conciliation is often used in employment disputes before they go to employment tribunals.

6. **What are some key elements that should be considered when resolving issues in the workplace?**
Some key elements include understanding the exact nature of the problem, the people involved, and the issue's impact on the workplace. It is also important to consider any relevant employment laws or company policies and to ensure that any resolution process is fair and transparent

7. **What methods prevent common employment law issues?**
Regular training sessions on workplace rights and responsibilities, transparent and fair company policies, effective communication channels, and a culture of respect and understanding can all help prevent employment law issues. Regular reviews of employment contracts and procedures to ensure they are up-to-date with current law is also beneficial.

8. **How can negotiation skills be improved for better communication in the workplace?**
Improving negotiation skills can involve understanding the needs and perspectives of others, practising active listening, expressing your own needs clearly and assertively, and learning to compromise. Training courses and workshops can provide helpful techniques and practice scenarios.

9. **What is the mediation process for employment disputes?**
The process usually starts with both parties agreeing to mediation. A neutral mediator is then selected. The mediator meets with each party separately to understand their views and then brings them together to discuss possible solutions. The goal is to reach a mutually acceptable solution. The mediator does not make decisions but facilitates the conversation and helps parties explore solutions

10. **Can an employee refuse to participate in conciliation?**
Yes, conciliation is voluntary in the UK, and an employee can choose not to participate. However, resolving disputes without requiring a tribunal is often a helpful step. If conciliation is not unsuccessful or refused, the dispute may proceed to an employment tribunal.

**COMPARE YOUR ANSWERS**
These answers are for the questions at the end of Chapter 6 on pages 96-99.

# TEST YOURSELF ANSWERS - CHAPTER 7

1. **What is an employment tribunal, and when might someone use one?**
An employment tribunal is a legal body that adjudicates disputes between employers and employees over employment rights in the UK. A person might need an employment tribunal if they believe their employer has treated them unfairly, for example, in unfair dismissal, discrimination, wage disputes, or redundancy issues.

2. **How does the employment tribunal process work?**
The employment tribunal process typically begins when an employee submits a claim form (ET1) outlining the nature of their dispute. The employer then has 28 days to respond (using form ET3). Afterwards, the tribunal may arrange a preliminary hearing to clarify issues and set timetables. The final hearing will occur, where both parties can present their case. After considering all evidence, the tribunal will make a decision.

3. **What can be the possible outcomes of an employment tribunal?**
Depending on the nature of the case, the tribunal may order the employer to compensate the employee, reinstate or re-engage the employee in their job, or dismiss the claim if it finds it without merit. The amount of compensation can vary depending on the case. For instance, there's no cap for discrimination cases, but there is for unfair dismissal.

4. **What are the implications of an employment tribunal for an employer?**
Losing a case at an employment tribunal can have significant implications for an employer. Besides the financial cost of any compensation awarded, the employer's reputation could also be damaged, potentially affecting their ability to attract and retain talent. It could also lead to lower employee morale and productivity. The employer might also need to review and modify their employment policies and practices to ensure compliance with the law.

5. **Why should an employee consider attending an employment tribunal?**
Employees should consider going to an employment tribunal when they believe they have been treated unlawfully by their employer and all internal attempts to resolve the issue have failed. Reasons could include unfair dismissal, discrimination, wage disputes, or parental or leave rights issues. However, going to a tribunal should be a last resort due to its potential cost, time commitment, and emotional stress.

6. **Can anyone represent you at an employment tribunal?**
Yes, you can be represented by anyone you choose at an employment tribunal. This could be a legal professional, a trade union representative, a colleague, or a friend. Choosing someone who understands the process and your case well is vital to ensure you are effectively represented.

7. **How long does an employment tribunal process usually take?**
The length of an employment tribunal process can vary greatly depending on the complexity of the case, the availability of all parties involved, and the tribunal's workload. Generally, a simple issue might be resolved within 4-6 months, while more complex cases can take over a year.

8. **What types of evidence are used in an employment tribunal process?**
The types of evidence used in an employment tribunal process can include written documents such as contracts, payslips, emails, or letters, as well as verbal proof, which could be witness testimonies. Physical evidence, like photos or video recordings, can be used if relevant. The tribunal will consider all evidence provided when making their decision.

9. **What happens if an employer does not comply with the outcome of an employment tribunal?**
If an employer does not comply with the outcome of an employment tribunal, the employee can take further legal action to enforce the tribunal's decision. This might involve getting a court order to pay any monetary award. Non-compliance by the employer can also lead to penalties and further damage their reputation.

10. **Can the decision of an employment tribunal be appealed?**
Yes, both the employee and the employer have the right to appeal an employment tribunal's decision. This can be done if they believe there was a legal error in the tribunal's decision. Appeals are made to the Employment Appeal Tribunal (EAT) and must be filed within a specific timeframe, typically within 42 days of the decision. It is important to note that appeals can be complex and costly, so legal advice should be sought.

**COMPARE YOUR ANSWERS**
These answers are for the questions at the end of Chapter 7 on pages 108-111.

# TEST YOURSELF ANSWERS - CHAPTER 8

1. **How did the Autoclenz Ltd v. Belcher & Others (2011) case redefine the approach to determine worker status?**
   The Autoclenz case clarified that courts should focus on the reality of the relationship between a company and its workers, rather than just the wording of the contract. This case advanced the concept that the real terms of an employment relationship may not be the same as those that are written into a contract.

2. **How did the Bear Scotland Ltd v. Fulton (2014) case influence the calculation of holiday pay?**
   The case established that compulsory overtime should be included when calculating holiday pay. However, the ruling also limited the retrospective effect of this decision, meaning workers couldn't claim back for many years of underpaid holiday pay.

3. **How did the British Gas Trading Ltd v. Lock (2016) case expand holiday pay calculations?**
   This case ruled that holiday pay calculations should also include results-based commission. This decision expanded workers' rights to fair holiday pay, stating that workers should not be deterred from taking holiday due to reduced pay.

4. **How did the Donelien v. Liberata UK Ltd (2018) case address the employer's duty regarding disability adjustments?**
   The case concluded that the employer had done everything that could reasonably be expected to find out about any disability when the employer sought professional advice and consulted with the employee multiple times. It clarified the extent of the employer's duty in making reasonable adjustments for disability.

5. **What was the implication of the Dudley M.B.C v. Willetts (2018) case on voluntary overtime and holiday pay?**
   The case concluded that voluntary overtime should be included in holiday pay if it is sufficiently regular and predictable. This expanded the scope of what is considered 'normal remuneration' for the calculation of holiday pay.

6. **How did the Wilson & Others v. United Kingdom case impact trade union rights in the UK?**
   The Wilson & Others v. United Kingdom case was a landmark ruling that strengthened trade union rights in the UK. The European Court of Human Rights found that the UK had violated Article 11 of the European Convention on Human Rights, which safeguards freedom of assembly and association, including the right to

form trade unions. This ruling led to significant changes in UK law, ensuring that employees cannot be disadvantaged because of their membership in or activities associated with a trade union.

7. **What was the HMRC v. Stringer case's significant outcome regarding paid leave?**
The HMRC v. Stringer case was pivotal in establishing that workers are entitled to accrue paid leave while on sick leave and can carry over unused leave to the following year. This ruling set a precedent for workers' rights to paid leave, ensuring that illness does not deprive them of this entitlement.

8. **How did the Uber BV v. Aslam case impact gig economy workers in the UK?**
The Uber BV v. Aslam case was a landmark ruling significantly impacting gig economy workers. The Employment Tribunal ruled that Uber drivers are 'workers' rather than self-employed contractors. This means they are entitled to certain rights like minimum wage, paid holiday leave, and protection against discrimination, which has far-reaching implications for other gig economy workers.

9. **What critical decision regarding holiday pay was made in the King v. The Sash Window Workshop case?**
In the King v. The Sash Window Workshop case, the Court of Justice of the European Union ruled that workers should be able to carry over and accumulate this leave indefinitely if they are not allowed to take paid leave. This was a significant decision, reinforcing the importance of workers' rights to paid leave.

10. **How did the Pimlico Plumbers Ltd v. Smith case influence the status of workers in the gig economy?**
The Pimlico Plumbers Ltd v. Smith case was another significant ruling impacting the gig economy. The Supreme Court upheld that Mr Smith, who was contracted as a self-employed plumber, was, in fact, a 'worker'. This meant he was entitled to worker rights such as sick pay and holiday pay. The case highlighted the potential misclassification of workers in industries like plumbing or delivery services and reinforced the need for accurate employment categorisation.

**COMPARE YOUR ANSWERS**
These answers are for the questions at the end of Chapter 8 on pages 124-147.

# TEST YOURSELF ANSWERS - CHAPTER 9

1. **What is the potential future of employment law in the UK?**
The future of employment law in the UK is expected to be shaped significantly by factors like Brexit, technological advancements, and changing work patterns such as remote and flexible working. While the core principles of UK employment law are likely to remain, aspects related to digital rights, privacy, worker classification, and cross-border working may see substantial revisions in the coming years.

2. **How has Brexit impacted UK employment law?**
Brexit has significantly impacted UK employment law, as the UK is no longer obligated to follow EU employment directives. However, most existing laws derived from EU legislation have been retained in the immediate aftermath of Brexit. Still, there is a possibility for changes in the future. For example, there may be changes to working time regulations or alterations to discrimination laws.

3. **How have technological advancements impacted UK employment law?**
Technological advancements have significantly impacted UK employment law, particularly data protection, privacy, and digital rights. With the increasing use of AI and machine learning in the workplace, there are growing concerns about employee monitoring, discrimination, and bias. This has led to calls for new legislation to protect workers in the digital age.

4. **How has remote and flexible working impacted UK employment law?**
The rise of remote and flexible working, particularly in the context of the COVID-19 pandemic, has posed several challenges to UK employment law. There are questions about how to ensure health and safety at home, manage working hours and rest breaks, and protect employees' rights to privacy when working remotely. This has led to discussions about potential revisions to existing laws or introducing new ones to accommodate these changing work patterns.

5. **What are some of the key legal considerations for employers in the UK with the rise of flexible and remote working?**
Key legal considerations include ensuring a safe working environment even in a remote setting, managing working hours and rest breaks in line with the Working Time Regulations, respecting employees' rights to privacy and data protection, and avoiding discrimination in remote working arrangements. Employers also need to consider how to handle disciplinary and grievance procedures when employees are working remotely.

6. **What potential changes could Brexit bring to UK employment law in the long run?**

While the immediate impact of Brexit on UK employment law has been limited due to the retention of EU-derived laws, potential long-term changes could include alterations to working time regulations, TUPE, and agency worker rights. However, it is worth noting that any significant divergence could affect the UK's access to the EU market under the Trade and Cooperation Agreement terms.

7. **How might the advancement of AI and automation impact employment law in the UK?**

The rise of AI and automation in the workplace could lead to significant changes in UK employment law, particularly regarding worker classification, rights to privacy and data protection, and potential discrimination or bias in AI decision-making. There may be a need for new legal frameworks to protect workers in the era of AI and automation.

8. **What are the implications of remote working on the employment rights of UK workers?**

Remote working can pose challenges to employment rights in the UK, including ensuring health and safety in a home working environment, managing working hours and rest breaks, and protecting the right to privacy. Employers must ensure they comply with all relevant legislation, even if employees are working remotely.

9. **How has the UK government responded to the employment law challenges posed by COVID-19?**

The UK government has introduced several measures to address employment law challenges brought about by the COVID-19 pandemic. These include the Coronavirus Job Retention Scheme (furlough scheme), changes to Statutory Sick Pay, and guidance on health and safety for home workers. However, ongoing debates exist about whether further legal changes are needed to protect workers' rights during and after the pandemic.

10. **How might the rise of the gig economy impact UK employment law?**

The growth of the gig economy has notably influenced UK employment law, especially regarding worker classification and rights. Cases such as Uber BV v. Aslam have questioned gig workers' status, prompting calls for law changes to safeguard them better. Future alterations may further clarify employment status definitions and enhance rights.

**COMPARE YOUR ANSWERS**

These answers are for the questions at the end of Chapter 9 on pages 134-137.

# TEST YOURSELF ANSWERS - APPENDIX I

1. **What does the term "Statutory Rights" mean in UK employment law?**
Statutory rights are the legal rights protected by law. In the UK, these include the right to a minimum wage, the right to paid holidays, the right to not be discriminated against, and the right to receive a written statement of terms for your employment, among others.

2. **What does "Unfair Dismissal" mean in the UK employment law context?**
Unfair dismissal is a statutory right that applies to employees working for an employer for a specific time (usually at least two years). If an employee is dismissed for a reason that the law deems to be 'unfair' or if the employer does not follow a fair dismissal process, the dismissal could be deemed unfair in the eyes of the law.

3. **What does "Redundancy" mean per UK employment law?**
Redundancy is when an employer reduces their workforce because a job or jobs are no longer needed. Redundant employees are usually entitled to statutory redundancy pay if they have been with the company for at least two years.

4. **How is "Constructive Dismissal" defined in UK employment law?**
Constructive dismissal is when an employee is forced to quit their job against their will due to the employer's conduct. To claim constructive dismissal, the employee must prove that their employer has committed a severe breach of contract.

5. **What is a "Zero-Hours Contract" in UK employment law?**
A zero-hours contract is between an employer and a worker where the employer is not obliged to provide minimum working hours, and the worker is not obliged to accept any work offered. This type of contract is often used in sectors where the workload can vary greatly, such as in the hospitality or retail sectors.

6. **What does "Grievance Procedure" mean in UK employment law?**
A grievance procedure is a formal way for employees to raise concerns, problems, or complaints to their employer. The law requires all employers to provide a fair and reasonable grievance procedure and to act promptly and impartially when a grievance is raised.

7. **Can you explain what "Maternity Leave" is in UK employment law?**
Maternity leave is a period of absence from work granted to a mother before and after the birth of her child. In the UK, eligible employees can take up to 52 weeks of maternity leave. The first 26 weeks are known as 'Ordinary Maternity Leave', and the last 26 weeks as 'Additional Maternity Leave'.

8. **What does "Discrimination" mean in the UK employment law context?**
In the context of UK employment law, discrimination refers to unfair treatment of individuals based on specific characteristics, such as age, sex, race, religion, disability, or sexual orientation. This is illegal under the Equality Act 2010, even if employees are working remotely.

9. **How is "Whistleblowing" defined in UK employment law?**
Whistleblowing is when an employee reports certain types of wrongdoing at their place of work, which is in the public interest. This may include criminal activity, health and safety violations, or risk of environmental damage. The law protects whistleblowers from being treated unfairly or losing their jobs.

10. **What is a "Fixed-Term Contract" in UK employment law?**
A fixed-term contract is an employment agreement that lasts for a particular time. It is 'fixed' in that it ends on a specific date when a task is completed or an event occurs. Fixed-term employees have the same statutory rights as regular employees.

**COMPARE YOUR ANSWERS**
These answers are for the questions at the end of Appendix I on pages 152-155.

# TEST YOURSELF ANSWERS - APPENDIX II

1. **What fundamental rights does the Data Protection Act 2018 provide individuals?**
The Data Protection Act 2018 provides individuals with several essential rights regarding their personal data. These include the right to be informed about how their data is used, the right to access their data, the right to rectification if data is inaccurate or incomplete, the right to erasure (also known as 'the right to be forgotten'), the right to restrict processing, the right to data portability, and rights related to automated decision making and profiling.

2. **How does the Equality Act 2010 protect employees from discrimination?**
The Equality Act 2010 consolidates previous anti-discrimination laws into one. It protects employees from discrimination based on specific 'protected characteristics', which include age, disability, gender reassignment, marriage and civil partnership, pregnancy and maternity, race, religion or belief, sex, and sexual orientation. The Act also covers discrimination in the workplace, including concerning dismissal, employment terms and conditions, pay and benefits, promotion and transfer opportunities, training, and recruitment.

3. **What are some key provisions of the Work and Families Act 2006?**
In the UK, the Work and Families Act 2006 introduced significant enhancements to parental benefits. It extended the statutory maternity and adoption pay periods, introduced additional paternity leave, now replaced by Shared Parental Leave since 2015, and made parental leave arrangements more flexible.

4. **How does the Employment Rights Act 1996 protect workers?**
The Employment Rights Act 1996 sets out the statutory employment rights of workers and employees. This includes the right to receive a written statement of terms of employment, the right to not be unfairly dismissed, the right to a minimum notice period if their employment ends, the right to maternity, paternity and adoption leave, and the right to request flexible working.

5. **What does the Health and Safety at Work Act 1974 entail for employers?**
The Health and Safety at Work Act 1974 requires employers to ensure their employees' health, safety, and welfare at work as far as is reasonably practicable. This includes maintaining safe machinery and work systems, providing necessary information, instruction, training and supervision, and a safe working environment without health risks.

6. **What is the purpose of the Agency Workers Regulations 2010?**
The Agency Workers Regulations 2010 aim to ensure that agency workers receive equal treatment to permanent employees doing the same job in terms of basic working and employment conditions, including pay, working time, night work, rest periods and breaks, and annual leave after a 12-week qualifying period.

7. **How does the Employment Act 2008 support dispute resolution in the workplace?**
The Employment Act 2008 notably reformed the dispute resolution process in the workplace, repealing the statutory dispute resolution procedures introduced by the Employment Act 2002. Instead, it introduced a more flexible approach, encouraging the resolution of disputes in the workplace before they escalate to employment tribunals. The Act also gave powers to the Advisory, Conciliation and Arbitration Service (ACAS) to provide pre-claim conciliation.

8. **What is the significance of the National Minimum Wage Act 1998?**
The National Minimum Wage Act 1998 established a minimum wage across the UK. This wage varies based on the worker's age and whether they are an apprentice. The rates are reviewed annually by the government.

9. **How does the Public Interest Disclosure Act 1998 protect whistleblowers?**
The Public Interest Disclosure Act 1998, often called the 'Whistleblowing Act', protects workers from being treated unfairly or losing their jobs because they 'blow the whistle' on wrongdoing within their organisation. It provides a framework for making disclosures about malpractice in the workplace. It gives legal protection to employees against being dismissed or penalised by their employers as a result of publicly disclosing specific serious concerns.

10. **What is the purpose of the Trade Union Act 2016?**
The Trade Union Act 2016, aimed at ensuring strikes occur only due to a clear, favourable decision by voting members, introduces a minimum vote threshold for industrial action, additional requirements for public services, a review of electronic balloting, supervision of picketing rules, and measures regarding political funds.

**COMPARE YOUR ANSWERS**
These answers are for the questions at the end of Appendix II on pages 180-183.

# APPENDIX V
# CREDITS & SOURCES

# IMAGE CREDITS

**Images used under license from Unsplash:**

| **Page** | **Image Credit:** |
|---|---|
| Cover: | Alex Kotliarskyi |
| Test Yourself pages: | Martin Martz |
| 1 | Pranam Gurung |
| 3, 6 | Tomas Anton Escobar |
| 4-5 | Mariana Alves |
| 8-9 | Nomadic Julien |
| 11 | Tim Schmidbauer |
| 13 | Gregory Hayes |
| 15 | Priscilla Du Preez |
| 45 | Amy Elting |
| 50-51 | Cytonn Photography |
| 53 | Jeshoots.com |
| 57 | Kraken Images |
| 59 | Max Larochelle |
| 71 | Chris Kursikowski |
| 88-89 | Tim Gouw |
| 91 | Janko Ferlic |
| 93 | Dylan Gillis |
| 95 | Charles Deluvio |
| 100-101 | Benjamin Child |
| 103 | Caleb George |
| 107 | Jan Huber |
| 112-113 | Brandi Redd |
| 128-129 | Sigmund |
| 131 | Alev Takil |
| 138-139 | Joshua Hoehne |
| 153 | Joshua Hibbert |
| 158-159 | Eilis Garvey |
| 165 | Jaanus Jagomagi |
| 167 | Shane Rounce |
| 169 | George Ciobra |
| 171 | ahsanization |
| 175 | Ethan Rougon |
| 179 | Stephen Picilaidis |
| 184-185 | Luca Baggio |
| 188-189 | Akhilesh Sharma |
| 212-213 | John Michael Thomson |
| 216-217 | Centre for Ageing Better |

**Images used under license from Pexels.com:**

| **Page** | **Image Credit:** |
|---|---|
| 19 | monicore |
| 32-33 | antoni-shkraba |
| 79 | Pixabay |
| 83 | Cottonbro Studio |
| 173 | Suzy Hazelwood |

**Images used under license from Pixabay.com:**

| **Page** | **Image Credit:** |
|---|---|
| 73 | PICNIC-Foto |

Images on page 64-65 and 67 are property of The Bank of England and are reproduced in full compliance with the editorial use terms specified at https://www.bankofengland.co.uk/banknotes/using-images-of-banknotes/

# REFERENCES


Adams, Z., Barnard, C., Deakin, S., & Butlin, S.F. (2021). *Deakin and Morris' Labour Law.* Hart Publishing. ISBN: 978-1509943548

Armstrong, M., & Taylor, S. (2023). *Armstrong's Handbook of HRM Practice.* Kogan Page. ISBN: 978-1398606630

Aylott, E. (2022). *Employment Law.* Kogan Page. ISBN: 978-1398603950

Barnett, D. (2021). *HR Hazards.* ELS Publishing. ISBN: 978-1913925024

Cabrelli, D. (2020). *Employment Law in Context.* CUP. ISBN: 978-0198840312

Collins, H., Ewing, K., McColgan, A. (2019). *Labour Law.* Kogan Page. ISBN: 978-1108462211

Daniels, K. (2022). *Introduction to Employment Law.* Kogan Page. ISBN: 978-1398603783

Freedland, M. & Kountouris, N. (2012). *The Legal Construction of Personal Work Relations.* OUP. ISBN: 978-0199551750

Kidner, R. (2023). *Blackstone's Statutes on Employment Law.* OUP. ISBN: 978-0192858603

Lewis, T. (2021). *Employment Law. Legal Action Group.* ISBN: 978-1913648329

Marchington, M., Wilkinson, A., Donnelly, R., & Kynighou, A. (2020). *HRM at Work.* Kogan Page. ISBN: 978-1789664867

*National Minimum Wage Historical Data:* https://www.gov.uk/government/publications/20years-of-the-national-minimum-wage

Painter, R., & Holmes, A. (2015). *Cases and Materials on Employment Law.* OUP. ISBN: 978-0199679096

Parry, E., Morley, M.J., & Brewster, C. (2021). *The Oxford Handbook of HRM.* OUP. ISBN: 9780190861162

Pyper, D., Seely, A., Brown, J., & Powell, A. (2018). *Employment Status (Report No. CBP-8045).* UK Parliament. https://commonslibrary.parliament.uk/research-briefings/cbp-8045/

Reiche, B.S., Tenzer, H., & Harzing, A-W. (2022). *International HRM.* Sage. ISBN: 978-1529763744

Susskind, R., & Susskind, D. (2022). *The Future of the Professions.* OUP. ISBN: 978-0198841890

Taylor, S. & Emir, A. (2019). *Employment Law: An Introduction.* OUP. ISBN: 978-0198806752

Wallington, P. (2023). *Butterworths Employment Law Handbook.* LexisNexis UK. ISBN: 9781474323987

Cornwall Wildlife Trust
AdVMEDIA
Remittance Advice

# APPENDIX VI
# INDEX

# INDEX

## E

# INDEX

# INDEX

# INDEX

Printed in Poland
by Amazon Fulfillment
Poland Sp. z o.o., Wrocław

34973287R00127